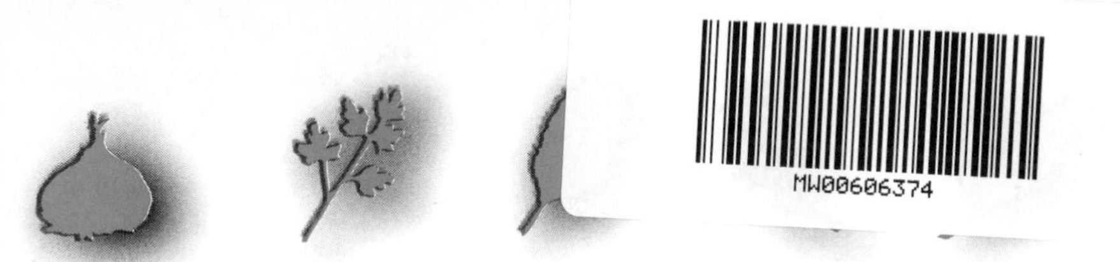

The Best of The Seasoned Chef

Compiled & Edited by
Susan Stevens, Director
The Seasoned Chef Cooking School

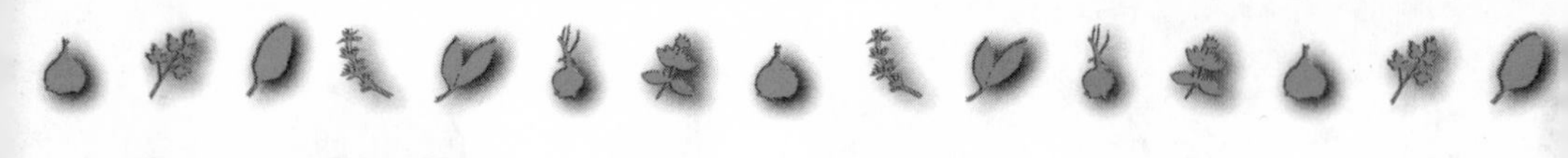

Additional copies of this book may be ordered from:

The Seasoned Chef Cooking School
999 Jasmine Street, Suite 100
Denver, Colorado 80220
303-377-3222
www.theseasonedchef.net
email: theseasonedchef@home.com

Please enclose $**24.95** plus **$3.00** postage per book

* Denver-Metro residents add $**1.85** sales tax per book
* Colorado residents *outside* the Denver-Metro area add $.**75** sales tax per book

You may also use the order form in the back of the book.

Published by The Seasoned Chef, Inc., Denver, Colorado, USA
First edition June 2001

Book design and graphics by Lynn Pike Designs, Golden, Colorado

ISBN 0-9708176-0-6

This cookbook is dedicated to the many fine chefs and instructors who have shared their culinary expertise, their exceptional talents and their passionate enthusiasm for cooking with many fortunate students at The Seasoned Chef Cooking School.

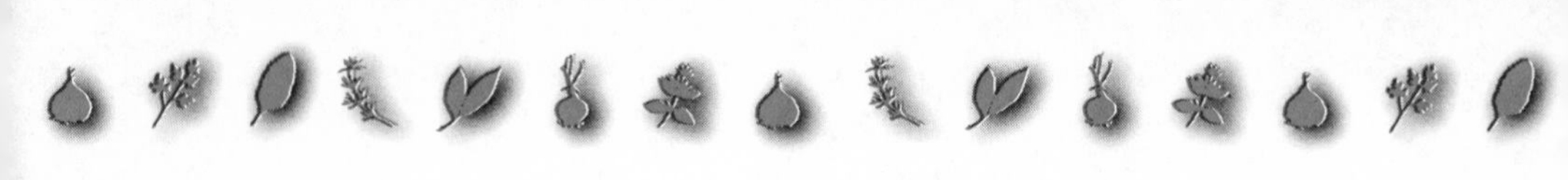

Table of Contents

Please bookmark our web site and visit often to see our exciting class schedule!

www.theseasonedchef.net

About The Seasoned Chef Cooking School

Since 1993, The Seasoned Chef has offered an extensive selection of exciting cooking classes providing expert instruction for the novice as well as advanced home chef. Classes are taught by experienced culinary instructors and chefs from local restaurants. Their expertise encompasses all aspects of food preparation from basic cooking techniques and knife skills to gourmet cuisine, ethnic foods, pasta and pizza making, bread baking, chocolate techniques, low-fat cooking, wine education and more.

Students learn in a comfortable and relaxed environment where they meet others who share their interest in fine food. In demonstration classes, students sample the delicious recipes as they enjoy watching the chef prepare an appetizing meal. In hands-on workshops, students work side-by-side and under the supervision of an expert instructor. Preparing and enjoying a delectable meal is proof of the new knowledge and skills that students acquire!

Please bookmark our web site and visit often to see our exciting class schedule!

www.theseasonedchef.net

About "The Best of The Seasoned Chef"

This book is a selection of just a few of the wonderful recipes presented in our cooking classes. It is not meant to be a comprehensive cookbook, but rather to present a sampling of the delicious culinary adventures experienced at The Seasoned Chef. A varied selection of exciting new recipes awaits both the novice and the "seasoned" chef.

The chefs and instructors who have contributed their delicious recipes are involved in all facets of the culinary industry from restaurants to catering to personal chef services. Each brings their unique perspective, their personal style and their singular talent to their signature cuisine. But they are unified by a passion for fine food and their generosity in sharing their time, talent and enthusiasm for their craft with appreciative students. This cookbook celebrates these exceptional culinary gifts and abilities.

Wine Notes

Wine pairings for various recipes were selected by Chris Rowe, Certified Sommelier. A frequent instructor of wine education classes at The Seasoned Chef, Chris enjoys sharing his knowledge and passion for this complex beverage with eager students. His thoughtful and pertinent wine selections will enhance your enjoyment of the delicious recipes.

Chef Talk

Chefs have a "lingo" all their own to expedite food preparation in their kitchens. When a cook is told to "sweat" the onions, it doesn't mean perspire while peeling, rather it means "cook in a small amount of fat, covered over low heat, until just tender". Woe to the kitchen novice who misinterprets this terminology as it could result in disaster, lost time and wasted ingredients.

Commercial recipes are often written using this terminology to simplify and shorten instructions for knowledgeable chefs and cooks who have been initiated into the mystique of "chef talk". But the home cook is often confused by these terms.

Here is an interpretation of a few terms you may encounter in recipes in *The Best of The Seasoned Chef:*

Blanch: to cook food, usually vegetables, briefly in boiling water, then immerse in cold or ice water to stop cooking. This process brightens and sets color, loosens skins (e.g. tomatoes, peaches) and partially cooks the food.

Caramelize: to cook (e.g. onions) until golden or well-browned, and starches have been converted into sugar, imparting a natural, slight sweetness to the food. Usually refers to melting sugar and cooking until deep, golden brown, but in current terminology also applies to other foods.

Chiffonade: thin strips or shreds of leafy greens or herbs (e.g. lettuce or basil). Roll the leaf tightly, then slice horizontally into thin ribbons.

Clarified Butter: used for cooking at high temperatures. Slowly melt butter (to evaporate most of the water); skim foam from the surface then carefully pour or skim off the remaining clear butter, leaving milky residue on the bottom. This clarified butter has a higher smoke point and doesn't burn as easily as whole butter.

Deglaze: to pour a liquid (e.g. wine, stock, water) into a pan in which meat has been sautéed or roasted in order to loosen the flavorful browned bits on the bottom. The meat and accumulated fat are removed from the pan first, then the liquid carefully poured into the hot pan. Cook, scraping up all the browned bits, until liquid has reduced slightly. This is usually used as a base for a sauce or stock.

Julienne: to slice into thin, match-stick size pieces (e.g. red peppers).

Reduce: to boil a liquid until thickened through evaporation. This thickens a sauce and intensifies flavor. Sauces are usually reduced by 1/3 and wine reductions by 1/2. Season after the mixture has reduced or it may be over-seasoned.

Sauté: to quickly cook food in a small amount of oil or other fat over high to medium-high heat; food should brown quickly on each side. Heat the pan first, then add the fat and heat again before adding food.

Sweat: to cook food (e.g. chopped vegetables, onions) in a small amount of fat, tightly covered, over low heat so it steams in its own juices and does not brown.

Appetizers

Appetizers

Asparagus in Phyllo-Parmesan Crust

John Schenk, Owner and Executive Chef  **JKS Culinary**

24 asparagus spears, woody ends trimmed
6 sheets phyllo dough, thawed
3 Tbsp. unsalted butter, melted
12 slices prosciutto, cut in half
4 oz. Parmesan cheese, grated

Steam asparagus for 2 minutes and chill in an ice bath; drain well. Preheat the oven to 450° with a rack in the center of the oven. Line a baking sheet with parchment paper and set aside.

Place a sheet of phyllo on a clean cutting board and brush lightly with melted butter; cut into 4 pieces.

Place one piece of prosciutto on one end of a phyllo sheet and top with an asparagus spear, leaving 1/2 inch of tip exposed beyond the top edge of the dough. Sprinkle with 1/2 teaspoon of Parmesan. Roll up and secure the edge of the dough with butter if necessary. Repeat with the remaining ingredients, transferring the rolls to the baking sheet. The rolls can be made 2 to 3 hours ahead up to this point, covered with plastic wrap and refrigerated.

Before baking, sprinkle the top of the rolls with remaining cheese. Cover the asparagus tips with foil to protect them from the heat. Bake until golden brown, 5 to 8 minutes. Serve warm, either whole or sliced into pieces.

Yield: 24 pieces

Artichoke-Olive Dip with Fennel Crudités

Conni Gallo, Chef  **Go Gourmet**

1	*15-oz. can artichoke hearts, rinsed, drained and patted dry*
1/4	*cup extra virgin olive oil*
1	*large garlic clove, crushed with 1/4 tsp. salt*
1/2	*cup brine-cured green olives, chopped*
3	*Tbsp. Italian parsley*
	Salt and freshly ground black pepper, to taste
2	*large fennel bulbs, trimmed and sliced 1/8 inch thick*
	Fennel fronds, for garnish (optional)

In food processor, purée artichoke hearts and olive oil until smooth. Transfer to bowl and combine with garlic, olives and parsley. Season with salt and pepper.

Place in serving dish and garnish with bits of fennel frond (you may use parsley sprigs instead). Serve with fennel slices.

Yield: 1 1/2 cups

Note: may be made one day ahead; cover and chill. Add parsley just before serving. Do not slice fennel until serving time.

Basil Pesto

Amy Hoyt, Owner  **Heavenly Baking and Catering**

"Delicious served as a dip, as a topping for crostini, used on pizza in place of tomato sauce or mixed with cream as a pasta sauce"

2 cups fresh basil leaves, packed
4 cloves garlic, peeled
1 cup walnuts
1 cup olive oil
1 cup grated Parmesan cheese
1/4 cup grated Romano cheese
Salt and freshly ground black pepper to taste

Place basil, garlic and walnuts in the bowl of a food processor; process until finely chopped. With motor still running, slowly pour in the olive oil. Add the cheeses and pulse until combined. Taste before adding salt and pepper.

Yield: about 4 cups

Note: pesto can be stored in refrigerator in airtight containers for several months, or in the freezer.

Bruschetta with Basil and Parmesan

Conni Gallo, Chef  **Go Gourmet**

1 1/2	*cups Italian parsley*
1	*cup basil leaves*
1/2	*cup walnut pieces*
1/2	*cup grated Parmesan cheese*
	Salt and freshly ground black pepper to taste
1	*baguette, cut into 32 slices*
	Olive oil

Preheat oven to 350°.

In food processor or by hand, finely chop parsley and basil. Combine with walnuts and Parmesan cheese. Season with salt and pepper.

Place baguette slices in single layer on baking pan and brush with olive oil. Spread 1 tablespoon basil mixture on each slice. Bake for 10 minutes.

Yield: 32 appetizers

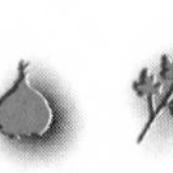

Roasted Red Pepper and Olive Bruschetta

Conni Gallo, Chef  **Go Gourmet**

2 large red bell peppers
2 cups Kalamata olives, pitted
2 Tbsp. Italian parsley, chopped
2 tsp. roughly chopped garlic
1 tsp. fresh rosemary, roughly chopped
Salt and freshly ground black pepper to taste

One baguette, thinly sliced and toasted

Roast the bell peppers by placing directly on burners over an open flame on the top of the stove, or in a 450° oven on a baking sheet, or over a grill. Turn the peppers often. until blackened and charred all over. Place in a paper or plastic bag and close tightly; leave to steam about 10 minutes.

Remove from bag and slip skins off. Cut peppers open and remove seeds and membrane; dice peppers small and set aside.

Place olives, parsley, garlic and rosemary into food processor. Pulse several times until olives are coarsely chopped and ingredients are combined. Turn into bowl and mix in roasted peppers. Season with salt and pepper. Mound onto toasted baguette slices and serve.

Yield: about 3 cups

Smoked Trout Toasts with Green Chile Pesto

Mary Clark  **Bluepoint Bakery**

Pesto:

2	*garlic cloves, peeled*
2	*medium ancho chiles, roasted, peeled and seeded*
3/4	*cup pine nuts*
4 - 5	*Tbsp. olive oil*
1/3	*cup grated Parmesan cheese*
	Salt and freshly ground black pepper to taste
10	*pieces Orowheat thin-sliced white bread*
1	*smoked trout, skinned and boned*
2	*Tbsp. sour cream*
	Minced lemon zest for garnish
	Chopped cilantro for garnish

Place garlic, chiles and pine nuts in blender. Purée, stopping frequently to scrape down sides. With the motor running, add the oil in a fine stream. Remove from blender; stir in cheese and season with salt and pepper.

Preheat oven to 375°. Stack 3 slices of bread and trim crusts, keeping the slices very square. Cut each stack into fourths to make canapé-sized toasts. Place in a single layer on a baking sheet. Toast for 3 to 4 minutes on a side or until crisp. Cool and store in a sealed container. (These keep well for weeks.)

To assemble toasts: Cut trout into small pieces, 1/2 by 1 inch. Spread a generous layer of pesto on each piece of toast. Top with a piece of trout and a small dollop of sour cream. Garnish with cilantro and lemon zest.

Makes 40 pieces

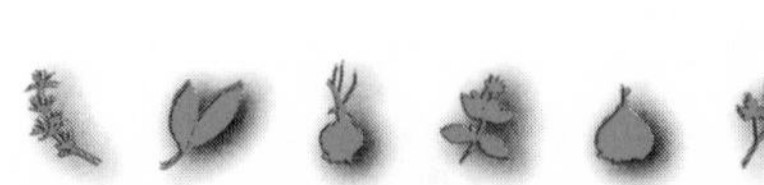

Guacamole

Norma Nuñez, Owner  **La Cueva**

4	*ripe avocados*
1	*medium onion, chopped*
1	*medium tomato, chopped*
2	*serrano chiles, finely chopped*
1/2	*lemon or lime*

Peel the avocados and remove the pits. Put all ingredients together in a medium bowl. Squeeze the juice of the lemon or lime into the bowl. Mash until you get the consistency you want (should be chunky). Serve chilled.

Serves 4 to 6

From: *Recetas de mi Esposo* by Norma Nuñez. Reprinted with permission

White Bean and Mustard Dip with Fried Wonton Chips

Cade Nagy, Executive Chef  **Paul's Catering**

1	*15-oz. can cannellini (white kidney) beans*
1	*clove garlic*
1/4	*cup whole grain mustard*
1	*tsp. lemon juice*
1	*Tbsp. grated Asiago cheese*
1/2	*cup olive oil*
	Salt and freshly ground black pepper to taste

In a food processor, purée beans, garlic, mustard, lemon juice and Asiago cheese. Slowly add olive oil while processor is running. Season with salt and pepper.

Yield: about 1 1/2 cups

Fried Wonton Chips

1	*pkg. wonton skins*
	Peanut oil for frying

Slice wonton skins into triangles. Pour oil in a skillet and heat until very hot. Add a few wontons at a time and fry until light golden brown. Remove and drain well on paper towels. Repeat with remaining wontons.

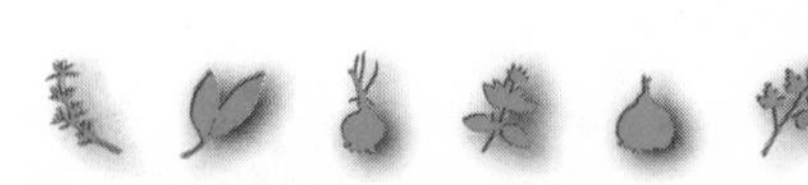

Beef Satay with Oriental Peanut Sauce

Cade Nagy, Executive Chef  **Paul's Catering**

1/2 lb. flank steak, well trimmed of fat
12 8 inch metal skewers

1/4 cup teriyaki sauce
2 Tbsp. soy sauce
2 Tbsp. rice wine vinegar
2 Tbsp. brown sugar
2 sprigs rosemary, leaves only

Slice flank steak into 1/8 inch strips across the grain; slices should be about 6 inches long. Thread onto skewers.

In a mixing bowl, whisk remaining ingredients together. Reserve 2 tablespoons of marinade. Pour remainder over flank steak and marinate in refrigerator for 1 hour. Drain well.

Grill over high heat until cooked to desired doneness. (Keep in mind flank steak toughens the longer it cooks.)

Oriental Peanut Sauce

1/2 cup creamy peanut butter

Mix 2 tablespoons reserved marinade with peanut butter. Thin with water as needed to make sauce desired consistency for dipping.

Yield: about 12 skewers

Chili Shrimp

Conni Gallo, Chef  **Go Gourmet**

1	*pound medium shrimp, peeled and deveined*
1/4	*cup olive oil*
1/4	*cup Italian parsley, chopped*
2	*large cloves garlic, minced*
1 1/2	*tsp. chili powder (or more, to taste)*
	Salt to taste

Combine all ingredients in a bowl; cover and marinate at room temperature for 1/2 hour. Drain oil from shrimp.

Heat sauté pan or wok and quickly sauté until shrimp is curled and pink. Serve immediately.

Serves 10 to 12 as an appetizer

China Town Chicken Dumplings with Chili-Soy Dipping Sauce

Andrea Alix, Owner and Executive Chef  ***Cuisine Chez Vous***

Filling:

1	*lb. chicken breast, diced*
1/4	*cup chopped green onion*
2	*Tbsp. <u>each</u> chopped garlic and ginger*
1/4	*cup soy sauce*
1 1/2	*Tbsp. chopped jalapeño*
1/2	*cup finely diced carrot*
1/2	*cup finely diced jicama*
2	*Tbsp. chopped cilantro*
1	*egg*
1	*pkg. gyoza wrappers*
2	*Tbsp. canola oil*
1	*cup chicken stock*

Filling: Place chicken, green onion, garlic, ginger and soy sauce in a food processor and purée. Remove mixture to a mixing bowl and mix in jalapeño, carrot, jicama and cilantro. Refrigerate filling until ready to use.

In a small mixing bowl, lightly beat egg with 2 tablespoons water to create an egg wash to seal dumplings.

To fill, place 4 gyoza skins on work surface in front of you and brush with egg wash. Spoon 2 teaspoons of filling into center of each gyoza skin. Pinch edges together starting from the filling and working out to edges to remove any air pockets. This should create a flat bottom and a ridge along the top. Place filled dumplings on a cookie sheet and cover with a sheet of plastic wrap. Refrigerate until ready to cook.

(continued)

Heat oil in a skillet on high heat. Place 8 to 10 dumplings in the skillet, being careful not to crowd the pan. Cook until dumplings are golden brown on bottom. Add 1/4 cup of chicken stock or enough to cover the bottom of the pan. Cover with a tight-fitting lid and steam dumplings until done, approximately 3 to 4 minutes. Remove from pan and serve immediately with Chili Soy Dipping Sauce. Repeat with remaining dumplings.

Serves 10 to 12 as appetizers

Chili-Soy Dipping Sauce

1/2	*cup soy sauce*
2	*Tbsp. rice vinegar*
2	*Tbsp. Chinese chili oil*
1	*Tbsp. minced ginger*

Place all ingredients in a plastic squirt bottle and shake vigorously before serving. To serve, squirt a small amount of dipping sauce on plate and arrange dumplings on top.

Citrus Cured Salmon Crostini with Ginger-Wasabe Sauce

Andrea Alix, Owner and Executive Chef  **Cuisine Chez Vous**

Salmon:

1/4	*cup finely chopped ginger*
2	*oranges, zested and thinly sliced*
1	*lemon, zested*
2	*Tbsp. pepper vodka*
2	*Tbsp. soy sauce*
1	*Tbsp. kosher salt*
1	*Tbsp. brown sugar*
1	*Tbsp. Szechwan peppercorns, crushed*
1/2	*lb. salmon fillet, skin removed (tail end if possible)*

Crostini:

1	*loaf French bread. thinly sliced on the bias*
1/2	*cup olive oil*
2	*Tbsp. garlic, minced*

Ginger-Wasabe Sauce:

1/2	*tsp. soy sauce*
1	*tsp. orange juice*
1/2	*tsp. lemon juice*
2	*Tbsp. pickled ginger, minced*
1	*Tbsp. wasabe paste*
1	*cup sour cream*
1	*Tbsp. finely chopped chives*
1	*bunch cilantro sprigs*

Salmon: mix together ginger, orange zest, lemon zest, vodka, soy sauce, salt, sugar and peppercorns. Lay out a large sheet of plastic wrap; arrange 1/2 of the orange slices on plastic wrap the approximate size of the fish. Coat fish with curing spices; lay fish over oranges and top with remaining orange slices. Wrap fish tightly with plastic wrap so it is well sealed. Place in a pan with a 5-pound weight on top (a bag of flour).

(continued)

Refrigerate for at least 3 days, turning once or twice a day. When ready to serve, gently wipe spices off with a damp paper towel and slice into paper-thin slices.

Crostini: Pre-heat oven to 350°. Mix together olive oil and garlic. Brush slices of bread lightly on one side and bake until golden and crisp, about 10 minutes. Set aside in airtight container until ready to use.

Ginger-Wasabe Sauce: In a blender mix together soy sauce, orange juice, lemon juice and pickled ginger; blend to a purée. Mix together wasabe paste and sour cream; add ginger purée and chives stirring to blend. Adjust seasonings to taste. Keep refrigerated until ready to use.

To serve: Place crostini on plate; spread with Ginger-Wasabe Sauce, top with a thin slice of salmon and garnish with sprig of cilantro. Serve immediately.

Serves 6 to 8 for appetizers

Italian Spanakopita

Dan Hayes, Owner and Executive Chef  **Campana Catering**

2	*cups chopped fresh spinach (washed and trimmed)*
3/4	*cup chopped artichoke hearts*
1/4	*cup chopped sun-dried tomatoes (oil packed)*
1/2	*cup coarsely grated mozzarella cheese*
1/2	*cup coarsely grated smoked Gouda cheese*
1	*cup feta cheese*
	About 1 cup olive oil, divided
	Salt and freshly ground black pepper to taste
1	*pkg. phyllo, thawed in box*

Preheat oven to 425°. Lightly coat a baking sheet with cooking spray.

Place spinach in a skillet over medium-high heat and cook briefly, until wilted. Cool slightly, then place in a bowl. Add artichoke hearts, sun-dried tomatoes, cheeses, 2 tablespoons olive oil, salt and pepper. Mix well.

Unwrap phyllo, lay flat on the counter and quickly cover with a slightly damp towel. Brush work surface with olive oil and carefully place one sheet of phyllo on oiled surface. Brush phyllo lightly with oil, then repeat with 2 more sheets. Brush one last time with oil.

Cut lengthwise into six 2 inch wide strips, then cut in half horizontally to make 12 strips. Spoon a small amount of the filling at one end of each strip. Diagonally fold pastry over mixture and continue folding "flag" style. This creates a triangle-shaped pocket of pastry with the filling in the middle. Repeat with remaining sheets of phyllo until all filling is used. (Wrap unused phyllo tightly and reserve for another use.)

Place triangles on baking sheet and bake for 17 minutes or until golden brown. Watch carefully to prevent burning.

Yield: about 30

Laura Chenel Goat Cheese Soufflé with Tomato Chutney

Kevin Taylor, Owner and Executive Chef  **Restaurant Kevin Taylor**

1/2	*cup water*
1/2	*cup (1 stick) butter*
1	*cup flour*
4	*eggs*
1	*lb. Laura Chenel goat cheese*
1	*Tbsp. grated Parmesan cheese*
1/4	*cup Crème Fraîche (page 198), whipped*
3	*oz. (5 Tbsp. plus 1 tsp.) cream*
4	*egg whites*
	Salt and freshly ground black pepper to taste

Bring water and butter to a rolling boil. Add flour all at once and whisk until thick and blended. Add eggs, one at a time, whisking until fully blended. Set aside.

With a mixer, whip goat cheese, Parmesan cheese, whipped crème fraîche and cream until smooth. Add flour and egg mixture, and continue mixing until fully incorporated.

Whip remaining 4 egg whites until soft peaks form and fold into cheese mixture. Pour mixture into 4 buttered ramekins to within 1/4 inch from the top of the dish, wiping carefully to remove any spillage. Bake in a convection oven at 425° for 10 minutes (or bake in a regular oven at 450° for 12 to 15 minutes). Garnish with Tomato Chutney and serve.

Serves 4

Tomato Chutney

1 *cup diced tomato (peeled and seeded)*
1 *clove garlic, sliced*
1 *shallot, minced*
1 *Tbsp. capers, drained*
1 *Tbsp. aged sherry vinegar*
1 *Tbsp. extra-virgin olive oil*
1 *Tbsp. basil, julienne*
Salt and freshly ground black pepper to taste

Combine all ingredients and bring to a boil for 2 minutes. Strain through a mesh strainer until liquid is removed and set aside.

Bring liquid back to a boil and reduce until almost evaporated. Add the tomatoes back into the reduced juices and adjust seasoning to taste with salt and pepper.

Cool to room temperature and serve.

Red and Green Quesadillas with Roasted Corn Salsa

Andrea Alix, Owner and Executive Chef  **Cuisine Chez Vous**

Roasted Corn Salsa:

	Olive oil
4	*ears corn, husks and silk removed, corn cut from cob*
1	*jalapeño pepper, with half the seeds removed, minced*
2	*cloves garlic, thinly sliced*
1/4	*cup finely diced red onion*
1/4	*cup finely chopped green onion*
1	*avocado, pit and skin removed, finely diced*
2	*Tbsp. cilantro, rough chopped*
	Juice of one lime
	Kosher salt to taste

1/2	*lb. spicy turkey sausage, casing removed*
2	*cloves garlic, chopped*
1	*onion, finely diced*
1	*Tbsp. butter*
1	*pkg. each red and green flour tortillas*
1/2	*cup shredded white sharp cheddar cheese*
1/2	*cup shredded queso blanco or Monterey Jack cheese*

Heat skillet with small amount of oil over high heat. Quickly sauté corn, jalapeño and garlic until corn is bright yellow. Remove from heat and let stand at room temperature until cool.

In a mixing bowl, combine red onion, green onion, avocado, cilantro and lime juice. Mix in cooled corn mixture. Season with salt.

Cook sausage for 3 minutes on high heat or until meat starts to brown; add garlic and onion. Cook until sausage is cooked through and onions are slightly caramelized. Drain on paper towels.

Lightly spread butter on one side of 4 red tortillas and 4 green tortillas. Mix cheddar and queso blanco cheeses together.

Heat skillet over medium-high heat. Place a red tortilla buttered side down in skillet; top with about 1/4 cup of cheese mixture and 3 tablespoons sausage mixture. Place another red tortilla on top, buttered side up. When cheese starts to melt and bottom tortilla is toasted, flip and cook other side. Remove to baking sheet and place in 200° oven. Repeat with remaining tortillas.

Cut warm quesadillas into wedges. Alternate colored wedges on a serving platter and place corn salsa in the middle. Serve immediately.

Serves 6 to 8 as appetizers

Smoked Salmon Quesadillas with Cucumber Salsa

Matthew Franklin, Executive Chef  **240 Union**

1	*lb. smoked salmon, thinly sliced*
6	*Tbsp. chopped red onion*
6	*Tbsp. capers, well drained*
1/2	*lb. jalapeño or dill Havarti, shredded*
6	*home-style flour tortillas*
	Salt and freshly ground black pepper to taste
2	*Tbsp. olive oil*
	Sour cream

Preheat charcoal or gas grill.

Place equal amounts of salmon, onion, capers and cheese on one side of each tortilla. Season to taste with salt and pepper. Fold in half. Brush with olive oil and place on medium hot grill for approximately 2 minutes per side, or until crisp and heated through. Remove from grill and let rest for 3 to 4 minutes. Cut in quarters and top with a dollop of sour cream. Serve with Cucumber Salsa.

Serves 6 to 8

Cucumber Salsa

1	*cucumber, peeled, seeded and cut into 1/4 inch dice*
2	*Roma tomatoes, seeded and cut into 1/4 inch dice*
1	*yellow pepper, cored, seeded and cut into 1/4 inch dice*
4	*green onions, thinly sliced*
2	*Tbsp. chopped cilantro*
1	*jalapeño, diced*
1	*lime, juiced*
1	*Tbsp. olive oil*
	Salt and freshly ground black pepper to taste

Mix all ingredients in a large bowl. Let rest 30 minutes before serving.

Yield: about 2 cups

Spiced Party Nuts

Amy Hoyt, Owner  **Heavenly Baking and Catering**

"Any nut can be used but I prefer either blanched almonds, pecan halves, walnut halves, or all three. This is a great party snack! Also, makes a thoughtful hostess gift"

1 1/2 tsp. salt
1 1/2 tsp. cumin
1 tsp. crushed red pepper
1 Tbsp. sugar

3 Tbsp. oil
2 cups nuts (unsalted)
1/2 cup sugar

In a small bowl, combine salt, cumin, red pepper and 1 tablespoon sugar.

Heat oil in a skillet. Add nuts and 1/2 cup sugar; sauté, stirring, until golden brown. Remove nuts from the oil and, while they are still hot, toss with the seasoning mixture. Store at room temperature.

Yield: 2 cups

Breads

Vanilla

Breads

Cinnamon Twists

Amy Hoyt, Owner  **Heavenly Baking and Catering**

1/2	*cup sugar*
1	*tsp. cinnamon*
1/2	*cup (1 stick) margarine or butter, melted*
1	*recipe Pizza Crust (page 39)*

Preheat oven to 400°. Combine sugar and cinnamon; set aside. Melt margarine in a small saucepan.

Pinch off golf ball-sized pieces of dough and roll into 12 inch lengths. Bring ends together and twist. Place on a baking sheet and brush with margarine. Bake for 15 minutes. While still hot, sprinkle twists with cinnamon sugar. Eat immediately!

Yield: about 15

Garlic and Cheese Grissini

Amy Hoyt, Owner  **_Heavenly Baking and Catering_**

1/2	*cup (1 stick) margarine*
6	*cloves garlic, finely chopped*
1	*recipe Pizza Crust (page 39)*
1/2	*cup grated Parmesan cheese*

Preheat oven to 400°. In a small saucepan, melt margarine with the garlic.

Pinch off golf ball sized pieces of dough and roll into 12 inch lengths. Bring ends together and twist. Place on a baking sheet and brush with margarine. Bake for 15 minutes or until golden brown.

While still hot from the oven, sprinkle with Parmesan cheese. Eat immediately!

Yield: about 15

Cumin-Pecan Corn Bread

Conni Gallo, Chef  **Go Gourmet**

1	*cup flour*
3/4	*cup yellow cornmeal*
2	*Tbsp. sugar*
1 1/2	*tsp. cumin seed*
1	*tsp. baking powder*
3/4	*tsp. salt*
1/4	*tsp. cayenne pepper*
1	*cup milk*
1/4	*cup canola oil*
1	*egg*
1/2	*large red bell pepper, cored, seeded and chopped*
2/3	*cup chopped pecans*

Preheat oven to 400°. Spray a 9 inch cake pan with cooking spray.

In a large bowl, stir together flour, cornmeal, sugar, cumin seed, baking powder, salt and cayenne. In a small bowl, whisk together milk, oil and egg. Pour wet ingredients into dry ingredients and stir until just combined (do not over-mix). Stir in bell pepper and pecans; pour batter into prepared pan.

Bake about 30 minutes or until a wooden pick inserted into center comes out clean. Remove from oven and cool in pan on wire rack for 10 minutes. Remove from pan. Serve warm or at room temperature.

Yield: one 9-inch pan

Irish Soda Bread

Amy Hoyt, Owner  **Heavenly Baking and Catering**

2	*cups white flour*
2	*cups whole wheat flour*
1/3	*cup brown sugar*
1	*Tbsp. baking powder*
1	*tsp. baking soda*
4	*tsp. salt*
1/4	*cup fresh rosemary, finely chopped*
1/2	*cup walnuts, rough chop*
1	*tsp. minced garlic*
1 1/2	*cups buttermilk*
2	*eggs*
2	*Tbsp. melted butter*

Preheat oven to 350°. Mix the dry ingredients together, then stir in the rosemary, walnuts and garlic.

In a separate bowl, mix together the buttermilk, eggs and melted butter. Add to the dry mixture blending all ingredients well. Turn dough out onto a lightly floured surface and gently knead by hand 2 or 3 times. Cut dough in half and shape each into a round loaf.

Place loaves on lightly floured baking sheet. Score the top of each with a cross pattern and bake for 45 minutes. Cool on a rack before slicing.

Yield: 2 loaves

Variation: this delicious loaf can be made into a sweet bread by eliminating the rosemary and garlic. Add 1 cup dried cranberries, currants or raisins and 2 teaspoons of orange zest. Great for turkey sandwiches!

Maple Sweet Potato Bread

Amy Hoyt, Owner  **Heavenly Baking and Catering**

3 1/2	*cups flour*
2/3	*cup sugar*
4	*tsp. baking powder*
1	*tsp. salt*
2	*tsp. cinnamon*
1/2	*tsp. nutmeg*
1 1/2	*cups mashed baked sweet potato*
1 1/2	*cups maple syrup*
4	*eggs*
1/2	*cup melted butter*
1/2	*cup oil*
1/4	*cup water*
2	*tsp. vanilla*
1	*cup chopped walnuts or pecans*
1	*cup dried cranberries or raisins*

Preheat oven to 350°. Coat two 9 by 5 inch loaf pans with cooking spray.

Sift the dry ingredients together. Beat sweet potato, maple syrup, eggs, melted butter, oil, water and vanilla together until well blended. Add to the dry ingredients and mix just until blended. Stir in nuts and cranberries.

Pour into prepared pans and bake for 40 to 45 minutes or until a cake tester inserted in center comes out clean. For muffins, bake at 400° for 20 to 22 minutes.

Yield: two 9 by 5 inch loaf pans or 2 dozen muffins

Pumpkin-Dried Cherry Bread

Conni Gallo, Chef — **Go Gourmet**

2	*cups flour*
1/2	*cup non-fat dry milk*
1	*tsp. cinnamon*
1	*tsp. baking powder*
1/2	*tsp. baking soda*
1/2	*tsp. salt*
1/2	*tsp. freshly grated nutmeg*
2	*egg whites, lightly beaten*
1	*egg, lightly beaten*
1	*cup canned pumpkin*
1	*cup brown sugar, packed*
1/4	*cup canola oil*
1	*cup dried cherries*

Preheat oven to 350°. Spray a 9 by 5 inch loaf pan with non-stick cooking spray. (Do not use a glass pan.)

In a medium sized bowl, whisk together flour, dry milk, cinnamon, baking powder, baking soda, salt and nutmeg. In a small bowl, whisk together eggs, pumpkin, brown sugar and oil. Add wet ingredients to dry ingredients and mix just until combined. Fold in cherries.

Transfer batter to loaf pan and bake about 1 hour and 15 minutes, or until a wooden toothpick inserted into the center of the loaf comes out clean. Cool in pan on a rack for 10 minutes, then remove from pan and cool bread completely on rack before slicing.

Yield: one 9 by 5 inch loaf

Note: Make sure your dried cherries are fresh; if they are old, they will be too chewy. However, you can soften them by soaking in water for about 30 minutes. Drain and pat dry before adding to the batter.

Parmesan Biscuits

Amy Hoyt, Owner  **Heavenly Baking and Catering**

4 1/2	*cups flour*
2	*tsp. baking powder*
1/2	*tsp. baking soda*
1 1/2	*tsp. salt*
1	*cup (2 sticks) butter, cold*
1	*cup shredded Parmesan cheese*
2	*Tbsp. chopped Italian parsley*
2	*cups heavy cream*
1	*egg beaten with 1 to 2 Tbsp. cream*

Preheat oven to 375°. In a food processor, blend the flour, baking powder, baking soda, and salt with the butter till the mixture resembles coarse cornmeal.

Place the mixture in a bowl and stir in the Parmesan cheese and parsley. Make a well in the center of the mixture and pour in the cream. Mix by hand to bring the dough together. Do not over-mix or knead. Roll the dough out to 3/4 inch thickness and cut with a round biscuit cutter. Place on a baking sheet lined with parchment paper.

Brush the tops with egg mixture for a glaze and bake for approximately 15 minutes or until golden brown.

Yield: 18 3-inch biscuits or 24 2-inch biscuits

Variations: replace the parsley with another herb, or a combination of herbs, such as basil, tarragon, chervil, dill or chives. Substitute another cheese, such as cheddar, for the Parmesan. Crisply cooked bacon crumbled into bits is another nice addition.

Tip: the smaller the biscuit cutter you use, the thinner the dough should be rolled or the biscuits will topple over when baking.

Turmeric Biscuits

Conni Gallo, Chef  ***Go Gourmet***

2	*cups flour*
1	*Tbsp. turmeric*
2	*tsp. baking powder*
1/2	*tsp. salt*
1/2	*tsp. sugar*
1/2	*tsp. baking soda*
4	*Tbsp. vegetable shortening*
1	*cup plain yogurt*

Preheat oven to 450°. Into a medium sized bowl, sift flour, turmeric, baking powder, salt, sugar and soda. Cut in shortening, using two forks, fingers or a pastry blender. Stir in yogurt.

Turn dough out onto a lightly floured surface and knead lightly, about 30 seconds (don't work the dough too much or the biscuits will be tough instead of light and fluffy). Pat dough 1/2 inch thick. Cut into rounds, using biscuit cutter or floured drinking glass.

Place on a baking sheet and bake for 10 to 12 minutes or until nicely browned.

Yield: about 12 biscuits.

Cornmeal-Pumpkin Seed Rolls

Conni Gallo, Chef — **Go Gourmet**

1	*cup cornmeal*
2	*cups warm water (110° to 115°)*
2 1/4	*tsp. dry yeast*
	Approximately 4 1/4 cups flour
3	*Tbsp. olive oil*
2 1/2	*tsp. salt*
1/2	*cup pumpkin seeds*
	Additional olive oil

Spray two 12 by 17 inch cookie sheets with cooking spray. Grind cornmeal in a blender, scraping sides of blender often, until cornmeal has a flour-like texture.

Mix 2 cups warm water and yeast in large bowl. Let stand until yeast has proofed, 5 to 10 minutes. Add cornmeal flour, 2 cups all-purpose flour, oil and salt. Stir to blend. Stir in 2 additional cups flour. Turn dough onto floured board and add pumpkin seeds to the dough. Using additional flour as necessary, knead until smooth and elastic, about 8 minutes.

Divide dough into 12 pieces. Shape each into a ball and arrange on sheet pans about 3 inches apart. Using scissors, snip an "X" pattern on the top of each roll. Cover with a damp, clean dish towel and allow rolls to rise until doubled in volume, about 30 minutes.

Preheat oven to 375°. Brush tops of rolls with olive oil and bake until brown and hollow sounding when tapped on the bottom, about 20 minutes.

Makes 12 rolls

Herbed Dinner Rolls

Gigia Kolouch, Culinary Instructor  **The Natural Pantry**

1/4	*cup tightly packed fresh parsley leaves*
2	*tsp. fresh thyme*
2	*Tbsp. chopped onion*
1	*large clove garlic*
2 1/2	*tsp. yeast*
1	*cup plus 2 Tbsp. warm water*
1	*Tbsp. olive oil*
3	*cups unbleached all-purpose flour*
3/4	*cup whole wheat flour*
2	*tsp. salt*
	Olive oil
1/2	*cup grated Parmesan cheese*
	Cornmeal

Chop the parsley, thyme, onion, and garlic together until finely minced.

Stir yeast into the water in a mixing bowl; let stand until creamy (proofed), about 10 minutes. Stir in the parsley mixture and 1 tablespoon oil. Mix the flours and salt together; stir 1 cup at a time into the yeast mixture. Stir until the dough comes together. Knead on a lightly floured surface, sprinkling with additional flour as needed, until silky and elastic, 8 to 10 minutes.

Place the dough in a lightly oiled bowl, cover with a damp towel, and let rise until doubled, about 1 to 1 1/2 hours. The dough should be soft and pillowy. To test if the dough is ready, poke it with a wet finger. If the hole fills in, the dough is not ready. If the hole keeps its shape, the dough has risen enough.

Punch the dough down on a lightly floured surface and knead it briefly. Cut into 8 pieces and shape each piece into a round. Brush each roll with olive oil and roll in Parmesan cheese. Place the rolls on a lightly oiled baking sheet. Cover with a damp towel and let rise until doubled, about 30 to 45 minutes.

Preheat the oven to 400°. Bake until the rolls sound hollow when you tap the bottoms, 20 to 25 minutes.

Yield: 8 rolls

Onion Buttermilk Rolls

Amy Hoyt, Owner  **Heavenly Baking and Catering**

2 1/2	*tsp. yeast*
1	*Tbsp. sugar*
1 1/2	*cups warm buttermilk*
2	*Tbsp. butter, melted*
1	*egg*
2	*Tbsp. minced onion*
3	*cups flour*
1	*tsp. salt*
1/4	*tsp. baking soda*
1	*egg, beaten*

Preheat oven to 375°. Sprinkle yeast and sugar into warm buttermilk; let stand for about 10 minutes for yeast to proof. In a separate bowl, mix together the butter, egg and onion and add to the buttermilk.

Sift together the dry ingredients and add to the above mixture. Beat on medium speed in a standing mixer with a bread hook for 10 to 15 minutes. (Or place in a bread machine and start cycle.)

Remove from mixer and place in a greased bowl. Cover and put in a warm place till the dough doubles in size, about 30 to 60 minutes.

Punch down the dough and turn out onto a floured surface. Roll into a rectangle about 12 inches by 18 inches by 1/2 inch thick. Cut lengthwise into 4 equal pieces, then cut crosswise into equal squares. Brush rolls lightly with beaten egg and place on a baking sheet lined with parchment paper. Bake for 30 minutes or until golden brown.

Yield: about 36 rolls

Pizza Crust

Amy Hoyt, Owner  **Heavenly Baking and Catering**

1	*Tbsp. yeast*
1 1/3	*cups warm water (110-115°)*
4	*cups flour (approximately)*
1/2	*tsp. salt*

Sprinkle yeast into warm water; let stand until yeast has proofed, 5 to 10 minutes. In a large mixing bowl, combine 2 cups of flour and the salt. Add yeast mixture and beat with a wooden spoon until smooth. Stir in 1 more cup of flour, then turn dough out onto a lightly floured surface and begin kneading. Add flour as needed so dough is not sticky; you may not need all of the flour. Continue kneading for 15 to 20 minutes, until dough is soft and silky. Do not add too much flour or dough will be tough.

Place dough in an oiled bowl and turn to coat surface with oil. Cover with a damp cloth. Place in a warm, draft-free place and let rise until doubled, about 30 minutes. To test, poke a hole in the dough with your finger; if finger hole remains, dough is ready.

Preheat oven to 450°. Divide dough in half and roll each into a circle. Form a rim around the edge. Place on a cookie sheet or pizza pan dusted lightly with cornmeal. Top as desired, then bake for 15 to 20 minutes or until crust is golden brown.

If using a pizza stone, place stone in the oven and preheat oven to 450° for 45 to 60 minutes. Dust a pizza peel lightly with cornmeal and place crust on peel. Top as desired, then carefully slide pizza from peel onto preheated stone. Bake for 15 to 20 minutes or until crust is golden brown.

Yield: 1–14 inch pizza; 2–12 inch thin crust pizzas; or 8–6 inch calzones

Topping Suggestions

- Quick Tomato Sauce *(page 205),* fresh mozzarella and fresh basil
- Roasted garlic, caramelized onions, olive oil and anchovies
- Mozzarella, fresh basil, tomatoes and olive oil
- Roasted peppers, olives and goat cheese
- Sautéed pears, walnuts and Gorgonzola cheese
- For breakfast: tomatoes, bacon, egg and cheese or grilled potatoes with onions and cheese
- For dessert: sauté apples with cinnamon and nutmeg; top with cheddar cheese

Pizza Dough Flavorings

- Reconstitute sun-dried tomatoes in hot water, then use the water to dissolve the yeast
- Chop 4 tablespoons fresh herbs (such as basil, oregano, Italian parsley, tarragon) and mix in with flour
- Knead into the dough chopped olives, roasted red pepper, lemon zest or chopped anchovies

Brunch

Cloves

Brunch

Christmas Oranges

Susan Stevens, Director  **The Seasoned Chef Cooking School**

"A Christmas morning tradition at our house. Serve in a glass bowl to show off the brilliant colors"

1/4 cup dried cranberries
1/2 cup Alizé® (passion fruit liqueur) or orange juice
4 large navel oranges

Combine cranberries and Alizé® (or juice) and let stand for about 30 minutes or until softened.

Meanwhile, peel and segment oranges. Cut a slice off of the top and bottom of the orange. Working from top to bottom, cut the peel and white pith cleanly away from the flesh. Follow the shape of the orange as you cut. Working over a bowl to catch the juice, cut between membranes to remove segments.

Add cranberries and liquid. Refrigerate for several hours or overnight before serving.

Serves 4 to 6

Stuffed French Toast with Mixed Berry Compote

Scott Elliott, Executive Chef  **Executive Tower Hotel**

"This is an easy, do-ahead dish when you have a crowd for brunch"

16	*oz. cream cheese, softened*
2	*pints fresh raspberries, washed*
	Sugar (depends on sweetness of berries)
20	*eggs*
2	*cups heavy cream*
3/4	*cup sugar*
1	*Tbsp. vanilla*
1	*Tbsp. salt*
1	*loaf Texas toast, sliced*
	Cinnamon and nutmeg to taste
	Powdered sugar

Preheat oven to 375°. Butter and flour a 9 by 13 inch casserole dish. Gently mix cream cheese, raspberries and sugar to taste; set aside.

Whisk together eggs, cream, sugar, vanilla and salt. Dip bread slices into the egg mixture and line prepared casserole with one layer of bread. Spread with cream cheese mixture. Repeat bread layer. Sprinkle with cinnamon, nutmeg and powdered sugar. Cover with foil and bake until firm, about 30 minutes.

Mixed Berry Compote

4	*pints fresh berries (your choice), washed and trimmed*
1/2	*cup orange juice*
1/4	*cup Grand Marnier*
1	*cinnamon stick*

Combine berries with orange juice, Grand Marnier and cinnamon stick; mix gently to combine. Let stand at least 3 hours to blend flavors. Remove cinnamon stick and serve over French toast.

Serves 12

Caramelized Onion Strata with Proscitto

Susan Stevens, Director  **The Seasoned Chef Cooking School**

3	*Tbsp. butter*
2	*large onions, peeled and thinly sliced*
1	*cup thinly sliced prosciutto*
1 1/2	*cups milk*
8	*eggs*
1/2	*tsp. chopped fresh thyme*
1/4	*tsp. dry mustard*
	Salt and freshly ground black pepper to taste
8	*cups cubed sourdough bread (preferably whole grain)*
1 1/2	*cups grated Gruyére or Fontina cheese, divided*

Melt butter in a large skillet and add onions. Cook over low heat, stirring occasionally, until golden brown about 30 to 45 minutes. In a separate skillet, sauté prosciutto until slightly crisp.

Lightly coat a 9 by 13 inch baking dish with cooking spray. In a blender or food processor, combine milk, eggs, thyme, dry mustard, salt and pepper. Blend until well mixed.

Combine bread cubes in a large bowl with caramelized onion and prosciutto. Pour in milk-egg mixture. Toss gently to coat bread cubes thoroughly. Spread half of the mixture in prepared baking dish. Sprinkle with half of the cheese. Top with remaining bread mixture. Cover and refrigerate overnight.

Preheat oven to 350°. Uncover strata and bake for 25 minutes. Sprinkle with remaining cheese and continue baking for an additional 20 minutes or until set. Serve warm.

Serves 8

Frittata Vera Cruz

Scott Elliott, Executive Chef  **Executive Tower Hotel**

1	*jalapeño pepper*
3	*Tbsp. butter*
12	*large shrimp, peeled and deveined*
1	*Tbsp. minced garlic*
1/2	*cup diced red bell pepper*
1/2	*cup chopped green onions*
	Salt and freshly ground black pepper to taste
	Pinch cumin
12	*eggs, well beaten*
1	*cup crab meat*
2	*tomatoes, seeded and chopped*
	Cilantro and lemon slices for garnish

Preheat oven to 350°. Place jalapeño in a small skillet over high heat and roast, turning occasionally, until skin blackens all over. Let cool, then remove seeds and veins. Chop finely.

Heat butter in a large ovenproof skillet. Sauté shrimp quickly on both sides. Add garlic, red peppers, green onions and chopped jalapeño; sauté for 5 minutes, stirring frequently. Season with salt, pepper and cumin. Gently stir in eggs, crab meat and tomatoes. Bake for 15 to 20 minutes or until a toothpick inserted in the center comes out clean.

Serves 4 to 6

Spicy Mexican Frittata

Scott Elliott, Executive Chef  **Executive Tower Hotel**

24	*eggs*
2	*cups milk*
10	*oz. chorizo (bulk)*
1	*jalapeño, seeded and minced*
1	*small yellow onion, diced*
1	*Tbsp. minced garlic*
1	*cup chopped tomatoes*
1	*cup grated queso fresco or Monterey Jack cheese*
1	*cup thinly sliced green onions*
	Sour cream and pico de gallo

Preheat oven to 350°. Whisk together eggs and milk; set aside.

In a heavy, ovenproof skillet, sauté chorizo until fat is rendered. Drain, leaving some fat in skillet. Add jalapeño and onion; cook until softened. Add garlic and cook until translucent. Gently mix in tomatoes.

Pour egg mixture into skillet; do not stir. Bake until cooked through, about 20 minutes. Remove from oven and top with cheese and green onions. Return to oven, if necessary, to melt cheese. Serve garnished with sour cream and pico de gallo.

Serves 12

Seafood Blintzes with Lemon-Dill Cream Sauce

Scott Elliott, Executive Chef  **Executive Tower Hotel**

Blintzes:

3	*eggs, slightly beaten*
1	*cup milk*
1	*Tbsp. vegetable oil*
	About 1 cup flour
1/2	*tsp. salt*
	Clarified butter, as needed

Whisk all ingredients together, except clarified butter. Cover and let stand at least 1 hour (preferably overnight) before using. Heat a small skillet over medium heat; coat lightly with clarified butter. Quickly pour in 1 to 2 tablespoons of batter, tilting pan to spread evenly. Cook until lightly browned on bottom. Remove to a plate. Repeat with remaining batter, brushing pan lightly with clarified butter as needed.

Filling:

6	*medium shrimp, shelled and deveined*
6	*large scallops*
1	*Tbsp. butter*
1	*lb. lump crab meat*
6	*oz. ricotta cheese*
1/2	*cup green onions, chopped*
1	*egg*
	Salt, freshly ground black pepper and nutmeg to taste

Sauté shrimp and scallops in butter. Add remaining ingredients, mixing well. Divide filling evenly between blintzes and fold.

(continued)

Sauce:

1	*medium shallot, minced*
1	*Tbsp. butter*
1/2	*cup white wine*
4	*cups cream*
1	*handful baby dill, finely chopped*
	Fresh lemon juice to taste
	Salt, freshly ground black pepper and nutmeg to taste

Sauté shallot in butter. Add wine and reduce until almost gone. Add cream and reduce by one-half. Add dill, lemon juice, salt, pepper and nutmeg. Serve over filled blintzes.

Serves 12 to 15

Salads

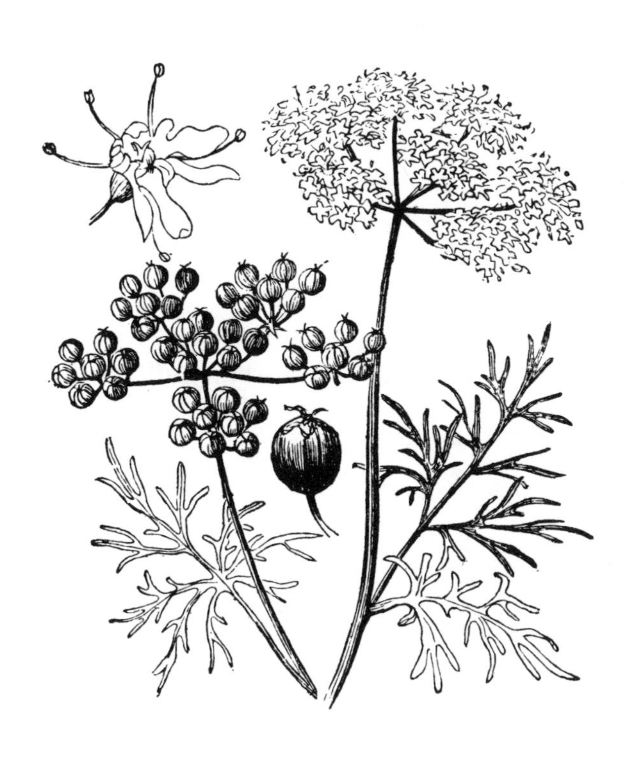

Coriander

Salads

Caesar Salad with Herb Croutons

Jan Leone, Owner and Executive Chef  ***janleone's***

This recipe won first place in the 1998 AIWF Caesar Salad Competition!

Herb Croutons:

	Day old French bread, cubed
1	*cup olive oil*
1/2	*Tbsp. dried basil*
1/2	*Tbsp. dried oregano*
1	*tsp. garlic salt*
1	*tsp. freshly ground white pepper*

2	*heads romaine, rinsed, drained and chilled*

Dressing:

1	*egg*
	Juice of 1 lemon
3	*cloves garlic, peeled*
12	*anchovies, packed in oil*
1	*tsp. Worcestershire sauce*
1	*tsp. Dijon mustard*
1	*cup olive oil*
1/4	*cup grated Parmesan cheese*
3/4	*cup shredded Asiago cheese*

Croutons: Place bread cubes on a baking sheet and let dry at least 1 hour. Preheat oven to 400°. Place in a large bowl. In a smaller bowl, combine olive oil, basil, oregano, garlic salt and white pepper. Drizzle over bread cubes and toss until well coated. Spread on baking sheet and bake until golden brown, 5 to 7 minutes. Use as many croutons as you like and save the rest for another salad.

(continued)

Tear or chop lettuce into bite-size pieces and place in a large salad bowl. In a blender, place egg. lemon juice, garlic, anchovies, Worcestershire and mustard. Blend well. Slowly add 1 cup of olive oil. Add Parmesan cheese.

Toss dressing with chilled romaine. Sprinkle with Asiago cheese. Add croutons and serve.

Serves 4 to 6

Note: If you are concerned about raw eggs, you may coddle the egg for 1 minute in boiling water before using.

Avocado-Grapefruit Salad with Tarragon Vinaigrette

Carol Ann West  **Chef**

Salad:

2	*ripe avocados, peeled, sliced and sprinkled with a little lemon juice*
1	*grapefruit, peeled and sectioned*
1/2	*small jicama, peeled and julienned*

Dressing:

1	*tsp. Dijon mustard*
1	*egg yolk*
	Squeeze of lemon juice
	Splash of Worcestershire or soy sauce
1	*Tbsp. chopped fresh tarragon*
1/4	*cup rice vinegar or light vinegar of your choice*
1/2 - 1	*cup canola or olive oil, or a combination of both*
	Salt and freshly ground black pepper

Arrange avocado slices, grapefruit sections and jicama on individual chilled salad plates.

Combine mustard, egg yolk, lemon juice, Worcestershire, tarragon and vinegar in a food processor and blend until smooth, about 20 to 30 seconds. Gradually drizzle in oil while the machine is running, stopping once in awhile to check the flavor. You may prefer it more or less acidic, so this part is important. Season with salt and pepper to taste. Drizzle dressing over salad and serve.

Serves 6

Note: If you are concerned about raw eggs, you may coddle the egg for 1 minute in boiling water before using.

Chayote Slaw

Greg Barnhill, Executive Chef  **Three Tomatoes Catering**

3 chayote squash
1 small red onion
1 red pepper, cored and seeded
1 yellow pepper, cored and seeded
1 green pepper, cored and seeded
2 Tbsp. olive oil, divided
3 Tbsp. lime juice
1/2 cup minced cilantro
3 Tbsp. sugar
Salt and freshly ground black pepper to taste

Cut the squash into thick slices and remove the seeds. Grill the chayote slices until softened; cool.

Julienne the onion and peppers. Sauté in 1 tablespoon oil over medium heat until softened. Remove from heat and cool.

When chayote is cool, julienne and add to the pepper mixture. Combine the lime juice, remaining tablespoon oil, cilantro and sugar in a bowl; add to the chayote mixture and toss to coat well. Season with salt and pepper; chill before serving.

Serves 6

Tip: wear rubber gloves to prevent irritation from chayote squash

Fennel and Grapefruit Salad

Conni Gallo, Chef  **Go Gourmet**

2	*Tbsp. olive oil*
1/4	*cup pine nuts*
2	*Tbsp. white wine vinegar*
1	*tsp. Dijon mustard*
2	*small pink grapefruit*
1	*medium-sized fennel bulb, thinly sliced*
2	*small heads radicchio, thinly sliced*
1/2	*lb. prosciutto, thinly sliced*

Heat a small sauté pan and add oil. When oil is warm, add pine nuts and crush with the back of a fork until finely chopped. Remove pan from heat and whisk in vinegar and mustard; set aside.

Cut peel from grapefruit removing as much white pith as possible. Cut sections free from membrane. In a bowl, toss together grapefruit segments, fennel and radicchio with the vinaigrette. To serve, arrange prosciutto on 4 serving plates and top with the salad.

Serves 4

Herb Vinaigrette with Mixed Baby Greens

Theo Roe, Executive Chef  **Dazzle Restaurant and Lounge**

2	*Tbsp. olive oil*
3	*Tbsp. minced garlic*
3	*Tbsp. minced shallots*
2	*cups extra virgin olive oil*
2	*cups pure olive oil*
5	*oz. (1/2 cup plus 2 Tbsp.) red wine vinegar*
5	*oz. (1/2 cup plus 2 Tbsp.) balsamic vinegar*
2	*tsp. kosher salt*
2	*tsp. black peppercorns*
1/2	*cup parsley stems, chopped*
1/4	*cup fresh oregano, chopped*
1/4	*cup fresh tarragon, chopped*
1/4	*cup fresh basil, chopped*
	Mixed baby greens

Heat a small sauté pan over medium heat. Add 2 Tbsp. of olive oil, the garlic and shallots. Reduce heat to low and cover the pan tightly. Cook the garlic and shallot mixture until translucent and tender, about 5 to 10 minutes.

In a bowl or storage container, mix the cooked garlic-shallot mixture with the remaining ingredients. Cover and store at room temperature for three days for flavors to blend. Strain and refrigerate.

Serve over mixed baby greens.

Yield: about 5 1/4 cups

Jicama, Orange and Grilled Onion Salad

Conni Gallo, Chef  **Go Gourmet**

1 1/2	*lbs. sweet onions*
2	*Tbsp. olive oil*
	Salt
1	*garlic clove, halved*
2	*blood oranges or navel oranges*
I	*medium jicama (about 1 lb.), peeled and julienned*
I	*cup cilantro leaves*
2	*Tbsp. lime juice*
1	*Tbsp. balsamic vinegar*
	Freshly ground black pepper

Slice onions 1/4 inch thick. Brush with 1 tablespoon olive oil and lightly salt. Grill onions until they begin to char and soften.

While onions are grilling, rub a serving bowl with the halved garlic. Cut peel from orange, removing as much white pith as possible. Cut sections free from membrane over serving bowl (to catch any juice), and add to bowl along with the jicama and cooked onions.

Add the remaining ingredients to the bowl, season with salt and pepper; toss thoroughly. Best when served at room temperature.

Serves 6

Mariachi Salad

Andrea Alix, Owner and Executive Chef  **Cuisine Chez Vous**

1	*ruby red grapefruit*
2	*cups jicama, thin julienne strips*
1/4	*cup red onion, thinly sliced and rinsed in cold water*
1/4	*cup radishes, thinly sliced*
2	*Tbsp. red wine vinegar*
2	*Tbsp. basil, chiffonade*
1	*ripe avocado, peeled and thinly sliced*
2	*cups shredded romaine lettuce*
	Kosher salt to taste

Cut peel from grapefruit removing as much white pith as possible. Cut sections free from membrane over a bowl to catch as much juice as possible.

Mix together grapefruit segments, juice, jicama, red onion, radishes, vinegar and basil. Mix in sliced avocado and romaine. Season with salt and serve immediately.

Serves 4

Pineapple and Jicama Salad with Cilantro Vinaigrette

Conni Gallo, Chef  **Go Gourmet**

2/3	*cup canola oil*
6	*Tbsp. white wine vinegar*
2	*Tbsp. minced shallots*
1/2	*cup cilantro, chopped*
1/2	*tsp. ground cumin*
	Salt and freshly ground black pepper, to taste
12	*oz. cleaned and trimmed baby spinach*
1	*medium jicama, peeled and cut into 3 inch julienne*
2	*cups cubed fresh pineapple*
1	*cup whole cilantro leaves (no stems!)*

In a small bowl, whisk together oil, vinegar, shallots, cilantro and cumin. Season with salt and pepper; set aside.

In a large bowl, combine remaining ingredients. Add dressing a little at a time, tossing to coat salad. (You may not have to use all of the vinaigrette.)

Serves 8

Seared Portobello Salad

Greg Barnhill, Executive Chef  **Three Tomatoes Catering**

Balsamic Syrup:

4	*cups balsamic vinegar*

Dressing:

1	*cup extra virgin olive oil*
1/4	*cup balsamic vinegar*
1/4	*cup minced fresh basil*
1/2	*tsp. minced garlic*

6	*large portobello mushrooms, stemmed and gills removed*
	Olive oil
	Salt and freshly ground black pepper

6	*cups baby greens*
2	*red tomatoes, sliced 1/4 inch thick*
2	*yellow tomatoes, sliced 1/4 inch thick*
1	*lb. fresh mozzarella (ovaline size), sliced 1/4 inch thick*

Balsamic Syrup: Over very low heat, slowly reduce 4 cups balsamic vinegar to 1 cup. This may take an hour or more. Cool to room temperature.

Dressing: Combine dressing ingredients in a blender and blend until emulsified.

Preheat oven to 400°. Brush portobellos with olive oil; season with salt and pepper. Coat a skillet with a thin film of olive oil. Sear mushrooms, top side first, for 1 minute; turn and cook 1 more minute. Remove to a baking sheet and roast in the oven for 2 to 5 minutes. Cool slightly, then slice.

Mix greens with dressing and arrange on plates. Surround with tomato and cheese slices. Drizzle with about 1 tablespoon Balsamic Syrup. Top with mushroom slices.

Serves 6

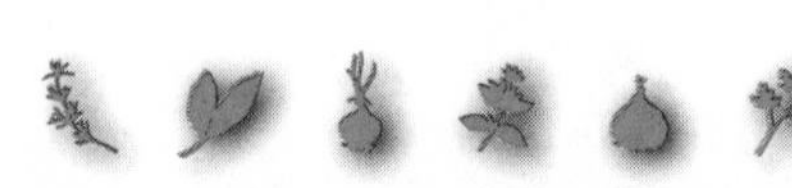

Wild Greens Salad with Hazelnut-Citrus Vinaigrette

Gigia Kolouch, Culinary Instructor  **The Natural Pantry**

Vinaigrette:

- *1/4 cup hazelnuts*
- *1/4 cup walnut oil*
- *3 Tbsp. orange juice*
- *2 Tbsp. lemon juice*
- *1 Tbsp. Dijon mustard*
- *1 Tbsp. orange zest*
- *1/2 tsp. thyme*
- *Salt and freshly ground black pepper to taste*

Spread hazelnuts on a baking sheet and toast at 325° for 10 to 12 minutes, or until lightly browned. Spread warm nuts on a towel, fold the towel over the nuts and rub together to loosen skins. Coarsely chop the nuts.

Mix remaining ingredients together in a glass cruet and shake to blend well. Add nuts.

Salad:

- *1 bunch dandelion greens*
- *1 head radicchio*
- *1 bunch arugula*
- *1 bunch loose leaf or romaine lettuce*
- *8 oz. fresh strawberries*
- *1/4 cup balsamic vinegar*
- *2 Tbsp. brown sugar*
- *1/4 cup olive oil*
- *1 tsp. salt*
- *1/2 tsp. freshly ground black pepper*

(continued)

Fill your sink with water. Remove the greens from their stalks and add to the sink. Stir them around in the water to loosen the dirt. Let them sit in the cold water while assembling the rest of the salad.

Clean and slice the strawberries. Toss with vinegar, brown sugar, olive oil, salt and pepper.

Drain greens and tear into bite-size pieces. Spin them dry in a salad spinner or roll in a clean towel. Arrange on a large platter. Drain the strawberries and sprinkle over the greens. Pour the dressing over the salad and serve immediately.

Serves 4

Wilted Field Greens with Sautéed Mushrooms and Sherry Vinaigrette

Jan Leone, Owner and Executive Chef  **janleone's**

12	*cups mixed greens, rinsed and chilled*
1/4	*cup walnut oil*
2	*Tbsp. olive oil*
1/2	*lb. each white (button) and shiitake mushrooms, trimmed and cut into 1/2 inch slices*
6	*Tbsp. pine nuts*
2	*large shallots, sliced*
1/4	*cup sherry vinegar*
2	*Tbsp. fresh lemon juice*
1/4	*cup finely chopped chives*
1	*Tbsp. fresh thyme*
1/2	*tsp. sugar*
1/2	*tsp. salt*
1/2	*tsp. freshly ground black pepper*
4	*oz. blue or gorgonzola cheese, crumbled*
2	*Tbsp. finely shredded basil leaves*
12	*cherry tomatoes, halved*
1/2	*red onion, thinly sliced*

Arrange greens on serving plates.

In a large skillet, heat walnut and olive oils over high heat until very hot. Add mushrooms and sauté, stirring constantly, until they begin to brown. Add pine nuts and shallots; sauté 1 more minute. Add sherry vinegar, lemon juice, chives, thyme, sugar, salt and pepper. Stir and scrape quickly to dissolve browned bits on bottom of pan.

Spoon mushrooms and sauce over greens, dividing evenly onto each salad. Dot each salad with cheese to taste. Scatter shredded basil leaves, cherry tomatoes and sliced red onion over salads. Serve immediately.

Serves 4 to 6

Chicken and Almond "Waldorf" with Dijon Dressing

Ben Davis, Executive Chef  ***Tony's Meats and Specialty Foods***

Dressing:

2 Tbsp. mayonnaise
2 tsp. Dijon mustard
1 Tbsp. apple cider vinegar
1/2 tsp. brown sugar
Kosher salt to taste
Freshly ground black pepper to taste

1/2 cup blanched, slivered almonds

1 tsp. paprika
1/2 tsp. dried tarragon
2 tsp. kosher salt
1/2 tsp. freshly ground black pepper
1 Tbsp. olive oil
4 boneless, skinless chicken breast halves

2 Granny Smith apples
2 cups red or green seedless grapes, halved
1 cup sliced celery
1/4 cup crumbled blue cheese
Juice of 1/2 a lemon

1 Belgian endive

Combine the ingredients for the dressing and season to taste with salt and pepper. Toast the almonds in a dry pan until golden brown. Set aside.

Preheat oven to 350°. Combine paprika, tarragon, salt, pepper and olive oil in a small bowl and stir to mix well. Add the chicken breasts and turn to coat well with the seasoning mixture. Wrap the chicken breasts in foil and bake for 30 minutes. Remove and cool to room temperature.

Peel, core and cut the apples into 1 inch chunks. Combine with the grapes, celery, blue cheese and lemon juice. Mix the dressing with the apple mixture and stir to combine well.

Separate the leaves of the endive and arrange on individual plates or on a serving platter. Mound the apple mixture on the plates. Slice the chicken breasts into long slices and arrange over the top of the salad. Garnish with the toasted almonds and serve.

Serves 4

Greek Chicken Salad

John Schenk, Owner and Executive Chef  **JKS Culinary**

"This is also delicious as a sandwich filling with foccacia bread"

- *3 Tbsp. vegetable oil*
- *3 skinless, boneless chicken breasts, diced*
- *2 stalks celery, diced*
- *1 bunch green onions, chopped*
- *1/2 small red bell pepper, diced*
- *1/2 small yellow pepper, diced*
- *1 bunch spinach leaves, chopped*
- *8 Kalamata olives, chopped*
- *1 Tbsp. capers, chopped*
- *1 Tbsp. Italian parsley, chopped*
- *2 tsp. fresh oregano, chopped*
- *1 tsp. fresh thyme, chopped*
- *1/4 cup Greek feta cheese, crumbled*
- *3 Tbsp. red wine vinegar*
- *1/4 cup extra virgin olive oil*
- *1 Tbsp. lemon juice*
- *1 Tbsp. lemon zest*
- *Salt and freshly ground black pepper, to taste*

In a heavy skillet, heat 1 tablespoon vegetable oil. Sauté diced chicken in small batches until browned. Remove each batch to a stainless bowl and cover to finish cooking. When all chicken is sautéed, let cool to room temperature.

While chicken is cooling, toss the remaining ingredients together in a large mixing bowl and season with salt and pepper. Add room temperature chicken and toss until well combined. Chill before serving.

Serves 8

Grilled Diver Scallops over Herb Salad

Greg Barnhill, Executive Chef  **Three Tomatoes Catering**

Vinaigrette:

2	*cups olive oil*
1/2	*cup champagne vinegar*
1/2	*cup chopped fresh herbs (your choice)*
2	*tsp. minced shallots*
2	*tsp. minced garlic*
	Salt and freshly ground black pepper to taste

2	*Tbsp. whole coriander seeds*
1	*Tbsp. kosher salt*
1	*Tbsp. black peppercorns*
18	*Diver scallops*
	Olive oil
	Salad greens

Vinaigrette: In a medium bowl, whisk together oil and vinegar. Stir in herbs, shallots and garlic. Season to taste with salt and pepper.

In a coffee mill, grind coriander seeds, salt and peppercorns. Dredge scallops in mixture. Heat olive oil in a sauté pan and sear scallops to medium-rare, 2 1/2 to 3 minutes per side.

Toss greens with Vinaigrette and arrange on a serving plate; top with 3 scallops per serving.

Serves 6

Nothing bring out the flavor of scallops like a great dry sparkling wine. The crisp acidity and the toasty components of Champagne make it an ideal match. Try the Veuve Cliquot gold Label (the vintage dated selection) from France.

Fusilli Salad with Feta

Amy Hoyt, Owner  **Heavenly Baking and Catering**

"This salad is a lovely accompaniment to grilled meat, chicken or vegetables"

2	*cups broccoli florets*
8	*oz. fusilli*
1/4	*cup minced red onion*
1/3	*cup finely chopped sun-dried tomatoes (oil pack; drained)*
1/3	*cup chopped black olives*
1/3	*cup chopped green olives*
8	*oz. feta cheese, crumbled*
2	*cups fresh sorrel or basil, julienne*

Dressing:

1	*clove garlic, minced*
1/2	*tsp. salt*
3/4	*tsp. freshly ground black pepper*
3	*Tbsp. red wine vinegar*
1/2	*cup olive oil*

Blanch broccoli for 2 to 3 minutes or until just tender; plunge into ice water (to stop cooking) and drain well. Cook fusilli in boiling, salted water for 8 to 10 minutes or until al dente. Drain well and place in a large bowl with broccoli, red onion, sun-dried tomatoes, olives, feta and sorrel, mixing gently to combine.

Whisk together dressing ingredients and toss with pasta mixture. Salad may be served hot or chilled.

Serves 4 to 6

Note: this salad keeps well for 3 days refrigerated. If needed, add more dressing to moisten.

Shrimp and Caper Penne Salad

Amy Hoyt, Owner  **Heavenly Baking and Catering**

Salad:

1	*lb. shrimp, peeled and deveined*
1	*lb. pasta shells*
1/2	*cup capers, drained*
1/2	*cup minced red onion*
1	*cup grated Parmesan cheese*

Dressing:

3/4	*cup white wine vinegar*
1 1/2	*Tbsp. minced garlic*
1	*cup fresh basil, tightly packed*
2 1/4	*cups olive oil*
	Salt and freshly ground black pepper to taste

Salad: Cook shrimp in boiling, salted water until just pink and curled. Drain and chill. Cook pasta al dente; drain well.

In a large bowl, combine cooked pasta, chilled shrimp, capers, red onion and Parmesan cheese.

Dressing: In a blender or food processor, combine vinegar, garlic and basil; pulse until basil is finely chopped. With the motor running, slowly pour in the olive oil. Season to taste with salt and pepper. Combine dressing with salad, using just enough to coat well; you will have dressing leftover.

Serves 6 to 8

New Potato Salad Dijon

Cade Nagy, Executive Chef  **Paul's Catering**

5 *lbs. new potatoes, scrubbed*
1/4 *cup salt*
1 *cup diced celery*
5 *hardboiled eggs, peeled and diced*

Dressing:
1/2 *cup mayonnaise*
1 *Tbsp. Dijon mustard*
1/2 *cup sweet pickle relish*
1 *tsp. garlic powder*
Salt and freshly ground black pepper to taste

Cut potatoes into 1 1/2 inch pieces. Place in a large pot and add water to cover by 3 inches; add salt. Bring to a rolling boil and cook until potatoes can be easily pierced with a fork. Drain and cool in cold water (an ice bath to shock potatoes is even better). Drain again.

Dressing: Combine all ingredients, mixing well. In a serving bowl, combine potatoes, celery and diced eggs with dressing. Chill before serving.

Serves 10

Soups
Rosemary

Soups

Chilled Strawberry Soup

Jan Leone, Owner and Executive Chef  **janleone's**

"Glass bowls are nice to serve in to show off the color of this soup"

1	*qt. strawberries, washed and hulled*
1	*cup heavy cream*
1	*cup plain or vanilla yogurt*
1/2	*cup orange juice*
1/4	*cup Grand Marnier (optional)*
3 - 4	*Tbsp. sugar (to taste)*
1/4	*cup fresh mint leaves*
	Sour cream for garnish
6	*mint springs for garnish*

Place berries, cream, yogurt, orange juice, Grand Marnier, sugar and 1/4 cup mint leaves in a blender (you may have to do this in two batches). Blend in short bursts. Don't over-blend or the soup will be frothy. Pour into a container and chill until ready to serve.

You may garnish with a dollop of sour cream or yogurt (plain or vanilla) and top with a mint sprig.

Serves 6

Asian Chicken Noodle Soup

Carol Ann West **Chef**

1	*package rice or cellophane noodles*
1	*Tbsp. sesame or canola oil*
2	*chicken breasts, lightly pounded, cut into thin strips*
1	*shallot, chopped*
2	*Tbsp. chopped garlic*
2	*quarts (8 cups) chicken stock*
1/2	*cup lemon juice or to taste*
2	*Tbsp. chopped cilantro*
2	*Tbsp. chopped parsley*
	Cilantro sprigs for garnish

Soak noodles in hot water until soft, approximately 5 to 10 minutes. Drain and set aside.

Heat a large soup pot; add oil and heat. Add chicken strips and sauté 1 to 2 minutes. Add shallot and garlic; sauté for another minute or two. Add stock and bring to a boil. Add lemon juice, cilantro and parsley. Stir in reserved noodles and leave on heat only long enough to heat through. Garnish with a spring of cilantro and serve immediately.

Serves 4 to 6

Chipotle-Lime Corn Chowder

Gigia Kolouch, Culinary Instructor  **The Natural Pantry**

3	*medium russet potatoes, peeled and cubed*
6	*cups water*
1	*14 1/2-oz. can vegetable stock*
1/2	*red onion, thinly sliced*
2	*chipotle peppers in adobo sauce, chopped*
2	*10-oz. pkg. frozen corn, thawed*
1	*Tbsp. mild chili powder*
	Juice of 1 or 2 limes, to taste
	Salt to taste
2 - 3	*Tbsp. chopped cilantro*

Place the cubed potatoes, water and vegetable stock in a soup pot. Bring to a boil, cover and simmer for 30 minutes or until potatoes are tender when pierced with a fork.

When the potatoes are cooked, skim any foam from the top of the pot. Add the red onion, chipotles, corn, chili powder and lime juice. Simmer for 10 minutes. Add salt to taste and garnish with chopped cilantro. Serve.

Serves: 4 to 6

Note: You may also use fresh corn on the cob. Slice the kernels from the cob before adding to the soup.

End of Summer Vegetable Soup

Matthew Franklin, Executive Chef  **240 Union**

2	*lbs. ripe tomatoes*
2	*Tbsp. olive oil*
1/3	*cup chopped onion*
1	*tsp. minced garlic*
3/4	*cup chopped zucchini*
3/4	*cup peeled and chopped eggplant*
3/4	*cup chopped red bell pepper*
2	*Tbsp. sliced fresh basil plus 4 to 6 sprigs for garnish*
1	*tsp. fresh thyme, minced*
2	*cups vegetable or chicken stock*
	Pinch of cayenne
1	*tsp. kosher salt*
	Freshly ground black pepper to taste

Peel tomatoes: plunge into boiling water for 30 seconds. Remove with a slotted spoon and immediately immerse in ice water until cool. Gently peel off skin. Cut tomatoes in half crosswise and squeeze them gently over a mesh strainer to separate seeds from juice. Reserve juice. Gently flatten tomato halves on a cutting board and coarsely chop into 1 inch pieces. Add to reserved juice and set aside.

Heat olive oil over medium heat in a 3-quart saucepan. Add onion and garlic; sauté for one minute. Stir in zucchini, eggplant and red pepper; sauté until softened, but not browned, about 5 minutes. Add tomatoes and juice, basil, thyme, stock, cayenne, salt and pepper. Bring to a boil; lower heat to a simmer, cover and cook until vegetables are soft, about 15 minutes.

Carefully pour soup into a blender or food processor and purée until smooth. (You may need to do this in 2 batches.) Serve hot or chilled garnished with a sprig of fresh basil.

Serves 4 to 6

La Ribolitta

Ben Davis, Executive Chef  **Tony's Meats and Specialty Foods**

1 1/4 cups dried cannellini beans
1 bunch Italian parsley (stems removed), chopped
4 cloves garlic, peeled and chopped
6 ribs celery, chopped
1 lb. carrots, peeled and chopped
4 medium red onions, peeled and chopped
4 Tbsp. olive oil
4 1/2 lbs. Swiss chard, washed and chopped
1 28-oz. can plum tomatoes, drained
2 loaves Pugliese bread, crust removed, sliced or torn
Kosher salt and freshly ground black pepper
Extra-virgin olive oil

Cook cannellini beans: place beans in a large pot and cover with 5 cups water. Boil for 2 minutes. Cover and let stand for 1 hour. Drain and add 4 cups fresh water. Bring to a boil; cover and simmer for 1 1/2 to 2 hours or until tender. Drain, reserving cooking liquid.

Sauté the parsley, garlic, celery, carrots and onions in the oil for approximately 30 minutes or until the flavors combine. Add the Swiss chard and cook for another 5 minutes.

In a food processor, purée 1/2 of the drained beans with the drained tomatoes and add to the soup. Add a cup or so of the bean cooking liquid to the soup. Continue to cook on low heat for another 30 minutes.

Add the remaining whole beans to the soup and enough boiling water to make the soup liquid but still thick. Add the bread and cook for 5 to 10 minutes more. Season with salt and pepper. Serve garnished with a generous amount of extra-virgin olive oil.

Serves 10

Pork Soup with Yams, Apples and Green Chiles

Carol Ann West  **Chef**

2	*lbs. pork tenderloin, trimmed of sinew and cut into 1/2 inch dice*
2	*yams, peeled and cut into 1/2 inch dice*
1	*medium onion, sliced*
3	*cloves garlic, chopped*
l	*4-oz. can chopped green chiles, divided*
3	*Granny Smith apples, peeled, cored and sliced*
2	*Tbsp. fresh oregano, chopped*
1/2	*tsp. ground cumin*
1	*cinnamon stick*
	Salt and freshly ground black pepper
1/2	*cup apple brandy*
4	*cups chicken stock*

In a soup pot, over medium heat, sauté pork until browned; remove from pot and set aside.

In the same pot, add yams, onion, garlic, 1/2 of the green chiles, apples, oregano, cumin, cinnamon stick, salt and pepper. Sauté for 5 minutes, then add brandy and chicken stock. Simmer for 20 to 30 minutes, or until yams are cooked through.

Add cooked pork and remaining green chiles. Simmer until pork is heated through; serve.

Serves 6

Sherried Mushroom Soup

Amy Hoyt, Owner  **_Heavenly Baking and Catering_**

6	*Tbsp. butter*
12	*green onions, finely chopped*
1	*lb. mushrooms, sliced*
3	*Tbsp. flour*
1/2	*cup dry sherry*
4	*cups beef or mushroom stock*
	Salt and freshly ground black pepper to taste
1	*cup half-and-half*

Melt butter in a soup pot and sauté green onions until wilted. Add mushrooms and sauté until soft. Sprinkle in the flour and allow it to absorb all the moisture in the pan. Slowly add the sherry and reduce until moisture is nearly gone. Add stock slowly, stirring constantly. Season with salt and pepper, and bring to a boil. Reduce heat and simmer for 10 to 15 minutes.

At this point you may blend the mixture to make it smooth, if desired. Return to the heat and add half-and-half. If you do not want to purée the soup, simply add the half-and-half at the end of the cooking time and simmer until heated through.

Serves 6

Variation: for a more intense flavor, replace part or all of the mushrooms with crimini mushrooms.

This soup will pair well with either red or white wine. When selecting the wine, consider the earthy tones from the mushrooms, the rich beef stock and the piquant flavor of the sherry. A full-bodied wine that will stand up to those flavors is a white Chateauneuf du Pape from Chateau du Beaucastel.

Shrimp Bisque

Conni Gallo, Chef  Go Gourmet

Shrimp Stock:

2	*Tbsp. canola oil*
1	*lb. shrimp shells (crab or lobster shells may be substituted)*
1/2	*tsp. chopped garlic*
1/4	*tsp. red pepper flakes*
1	*cup white wine*
1	*large red onion, roughly chopped*
2	*carrots, peeled and cut into 1/2-inch pieces*
1/2	*of a 6-oz. can tomato paste*
1/2	*tsp. thyme*
1/2	*tsp. tarragon*
2	*bay leaves*
3	*peppercorns*
2	*quarts (8 cups) water*

In a large stock pot, heat oil over medium-high heat. Add shrimp shells, stirring until lightly toasted. Add garlic and pepper flakes, and sauté about 1 minute. Deglaze pan with white wine and add remaining ingredients. Bring to a boil, reduce heat and simmer 45 minutes. Skim as necessary. Strain stock, discarding shells.

Bisque:

5	*Tbsp. butter*
1/2	*cup flour*
3 1/2	*cups Shrimp Stock*
1	*cup tomato purée (strain seeds, if any)*
1	*vanilla bean*
2/3	*cup heavy cream*
1/2	*cup dry sherry*
1/3	*cup veal or beef stock*
1 1/3	*cups shiitake mushrooms, thinly sliced*
1	*cup raw shrimp, shelled and roughly chopped*
	Salt and freshly ground white pepper

In large saucepan, melt butter over medium heat. Make a roux by adding the flour and whisking until smooth. Continue cooking to blond roux stage (lightly colored). Slowly whisk in cooled shrimp stock. Stir in tomato puree. Split vanilla bean and scrape inside of pod (seeds) into soup. Add pod to soup also. Stir in cream, sherry, and veal stock. Bring bisque to a boil, reduce heat and simmer without stirring for 10 minutes. Skim any foam that accumulates on top of the bisque. Add mushrooms and shrimp. Cook 2 more minutes; season to taste with salt and pepper. Remove vanilla bean pod and serve.

Serves 6

Full-bodied, rich and silky, a bisque is the pinnacle of all soups. Look to the home of Chardonnay—Burgundy, France— for the perfect match. A dry, full-bodied Chardonnay with hints of lemon and apple such as Louis Lature Chassagne Montrachet.

Sopa de Tortilla

Norma Nuñez  **La Cueva**

1 cup vegetable oil, plus 1 Tbsp.
12 corn tortillas

1 medium onion
1 tomato
1 fresh jalapeño
1 clove garlic, minced
8 cups chicken broth
Salt
8 oz. white (or yellow) cheddar cheese, shredded
1 ripe avocado, peeled and sliced

In a large skillet, heat 1 cup oil over medium heat. While the oil is heating, stack the tortillas and cut into 15 strips (about 1/4 inch wide). Place one strip in the oil to test the temperature. The oil should bubble around the strip slightly. If it bubbles too rapidly, the oil is too hot and the soup will taste burned. If the oil is not hot enough, the tortilla strips will be greasy. When you have reached the correct temperature, cook all the strips together until they are crispy. Remove from the skillet and place the strips onto paper towels to soak up any excess oil. Set aside.

Slice the onion, tomato and jalapeño into strips. In a soup pot, sauté the onion and minced garlic in the remaining tablespoon of oil. Add the tomato and jalapeño, and continue to sauté for 5 minutes. Add the chicken broth and bring to a medium boil. Simmer for 20 minutes; add salt to taste.

Immediately before serving, divide the tortilla strips into 4 bowls. Sprinkle 2 oz. of the shredded cheese into each bowl and fill with the broth. Garnish with fresh avocado slices.

Serves 4

From *Recetas de mi Esposo* by Norma Nuñez. Reprinted with permission.

Tomato and Fresh Basil Soup

Jan Leone, Owner and Executive Chef  **janleone's**

1	*cup diced yellow onion*
1/4	*cup each butter and olive oil*
1	*tsp. dried basil*
2	*cloves garlic, finely chopped*
2	*28-oz. cans crushed tomatoes*
1/3	*cup sugar*
1/2	*tsp. salt or to taste*
1/4	*tsp. freshly ground black pepper or to taste*
2	*cups cream*
1/3	*cup shredded fresh basil leaves*
	Fresh whole basil leaves

In a large saucepan, sauté onion in butter and oil for 6 minutes on medium heat. Stir in dried basil and garlic; sauté for 2 minutes more. Add tomatoes, sugar, salt and pepper. Simmer for 10 minutes. Add cream and heat to boiling point. Mix in shredded basil.

Serve garnished with whole basil leaves.

Serves 6

The creaminess of this soup calls for a sparkling wine to balance its richness and enhance the summery flavors. Taittinger Brut Rosé from Champagne, France is an ideal pairing.

Truffled Potato Soup

Chris Cina, Executive Chef  **The Fourth Story Restaurant**

2 Tbsp. butter
2 Tbsp. chopped garlic
1 leek, cleaned and sliced (white part only)
6 potatoes, peeled and diced
8 cups chicken stock (if using canned, be sure to use low sodium)
Juice of 1 lemon
Salt and freshly ground white pepper
White truffle oil to garnish
2 Tbsp. chopped chives

Melt butter in a medium-sized saucepan, add the garlic and leek. Cover and cook until soft, about 5 minutes. Add the potatoes and chicken stock. Bring to a boil, then reduce heat to a simmer and continue cooking until the potatoes are soft.

With a hand blender, purée the soup until smooth. Season with the lemon juice, salt and white pepper.

At serving time, drizzle the soup with white truffle oil and garnish with chopped chives.

Serves 6 to 8

This hearty soup deserves an equally hearty wine that can balance and compliment the earthiness of the potatoes and truffles. The Viognier from Arrowood Vineyards in Sonoma is up to the challenge. When grown in California, Viognier (a grape native to the Northern Rhone Valley in France) is well-balanced with apricot and spice notes, full bodied and a touch dry.

Wild Mushroom and Asparagus Soup with Brie

Greg Barnhill, Executive Chef  **Three Tomatoes Catering**

1/2	*lb. each shiitake, portobello and field (button) mushrooms*
1/2	*lb. asparagus, cleaned*
2	*cups mushroom or chicken stock*
1/2	*cup sherry*
2	*cups heavy cream*
	Olive oil for sautéing
1	*Tbsp. minced shallots*
1	*Tbsp. minced garlic*
1	*Tbsp. fresh rosemary, minced*
1/2	*lb. ripe Brie cheese, rind removed and cut into cubes*
	Salt and freshly ground black pepper to taste

Remove stems from the shiitake and portobello mushrooms (these may be used in making a mushroom stock). Clean dark gills off of portobello mushrooms. Slice mushrooms and set aside. Finely chop the button mushrooms in a food processor and set aside. Snap off tough stem ends of asparagus and discard. Cut off 2 inch tips of asparagus spears; set aside.

In a large stock pot, heat stock to a simmer. Add shiitakes, portobellos, asparagus stems and sherry. Simmer for about 1 hour. Purée soup in a blender or food processor then return to stock pot. Add heavy cream and simmer until reduced by 1/3.

Heat olive oil in a skillet and sauté chopped button mushrooms, shallots, garlic, rosemary and asparagus tips. Add to soup along with Brie cheese cubes. Season to taste with salt and pepper.

Serves 8

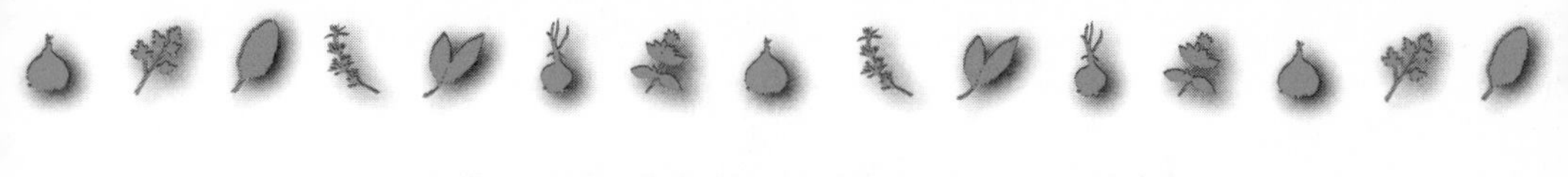

Meats

Meats

Basque Country Barbecued Ribs

Mary Clark  **Bluepoint Bakery**

"Be sure to plan ahead to make these great ribs as marinating takes 24 to 48 hours!"

4 lbs. country-style pork ribs

Marinade:

1 1/2 tsp. kosher salt
1 tsp. fresh thyme
1/2 tsp. fennel seed
1/2 tsp. chopped rosemary
6 mint leaves slivered
1 sage leaf, slivered
1 bay leaf
4 cloves garlic, sliced
2 Tbsp. olive oil

Herb Flavored Oil:

3 sprigs fresh thyme
1 bay leaf
1 tsp. fennel seed
2 sprigs fresh mint
2 sage leaves
1/2 cup olive oil

4 - 6 medium baking potatoes
Freshly ground black pepper
Oil for grilling
2 - 3 Tbsp. fresh lemon juice
Fresh herb sprigs for garnish

Up to 2 days in advance, mix Marinade ingredients and rub onto all sides of ribs. Place in a glass or enamel pan; cover and marinate in refrigerator for 24 to 48 hours; turn ribs occasionally. Mix together ingredients for Herb Flavored Oil and heat gently over low heat to just warm. Remove from heat and cool. Cover and set aside to macerate at room temperature.

Two hours before grilling remove ribs from refrigerator and brush off excess marinade. Leave at room temperature. Peel potatoes and cut into 1 inch thick slices. Brush potatoes with Herb Flavored Oil.

(continued)

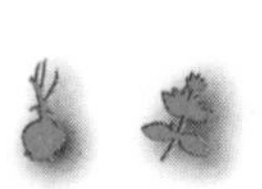
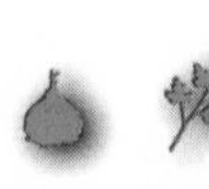

Pre-heat gas grill or barbecue. The grill should be about 8 inches from the heat if using charcoal and a bit closer for gas. Be sure the grill surface is broiling hot before beginning to cook. Rub oil on the grill and place ribs flat on the grill.

Every 10 minutes, turn and baste meat with Herb Flavored Oil. Add potatoes after the first 10 minutes. Baste potatoes as well. If meat or potatoes flame up or are browning too fast, move to a cooler spot on the grill and keep checking to cook over hottest possible spot without burning. Meat should be cooked well done, 45 minutes to 1 hour. (You may need to add charcoal about 20 minutes into cooking to extend the fire for enough cooking time.) Remove to a heated platter and serve with a squeeze of lemon and fresh herb sprigs.

Serves 4

Most rib dishes cry out for beer as the prefect beverage. This preparation, however, with its inherent heartiness, calls out for wine. A Spanish Rioja (the highest classified wine in the country) is a great accompaniment. With its layered flavors of dried fruits and full-bodied mouth feel, the Rioja from the Bodegas Monticello is an ideal choice.

Beef Short Ribs with Chipotles

Mary Clark **Bluepoint Bakery**

3 - 4	*lbs. beef short ribs*
	Salt and freshly ground black pepper
3	*Tbsp. canola oil*
6	*large Roma tomatoes, cored*
1	*small onion, peeled and quartered*
2	*chipotle chiles in adobo sauce, including a little sauce*
3	*garlic cloves*
1/4	*tsp. Mexican oregano*
2	*sprigs parsley*
1/4	*cup water*
	Salt and freshly ground black pepper to taste

Season the short ribs with salt and pepper. Heat oil in a Dutch oven and brown ribs on all sides, about 10 to 15 minutes. Pour off any extra fat and set pan aside, off the heat.

While meat is browning, heat a heavy skillet over high heat. When very hot, place whole tomatoes, stem side down, in pan and roast until skin chars. Turn and roast on all sides, about 10 minutes total, reducing heat as necessary to prevent burning. Remove to a bowl being careful to save all the juice. Add onion quarters to pan, roast and remove to the same bowl. In a blender, purée tomatoes, onion, chipotle chiles, garlic, oregano, parsley and water to a smooth paste. Taste and add more chipotle if you like a hotter sauce.

Pour the purée over the meat and return to medium heat. Cover and simmer the ribs very gently for 2 to 3 hours. This can also be done in the oven at 210° to 220°. When meat is very tender, remove the ribs. Skim the sauce of any fat. Taste and adjust seasoning with salt and pepper as well as additional adobo sauce. Serve.

Serves 4

Short Ribs with Sun-Dried Tomato and Dijon Mustard Sauce

Theo Roe, Executive Chef  **Dazzle Restaurant and Lounge**

4 Tbsp. vegetable oil
4 pieces beef short ribs
1 carrot, medium dice
1 onion, medium dice
1 Tbsp. tomato paste
1 cup red wine
4 cups chicken stock
1 head garlic, peeled and separated into cloves
1 sprig fresh thyme
1 fresh parsley stem
5 black peppercorns, crushed
1 bay leaf
Kosher salt and freshly ground black pepper to taste
1 Tbsp. each butter and Dijon mustard
3 Tbsp. sun-dried tomatoes, rehydrated and julienned
Chopped fresh parsley
Salt and freshly ground black pepper to taste

Preheat oven to 350°. Place an ovenproof sauté or saucepan in oven until hot, about 10 minutes. Place on burner over medium-high heat and add vegetable oil; heat. Add short ribs and sear on all sides. Remove when evenly browned and set aside. Add the carrots and onions to the pan and slowly caramelize (cook until well browned). Add the tomato paste and mix in thoroughly. Add red wine and reduce by half. Add the chicken stock and bring to a boil; remove from heat.

Place seared ribs into a roasting pan with garlic cloves, thyme, parsley, peppercorns and bay leaf. Season with salt and pepper. Pour the hot chicken stock mixture over the ribs; cover with foil and cook for 2 1/2 hours or until fork tender. When short ribs are done, carefully remove and place on a serving platter.

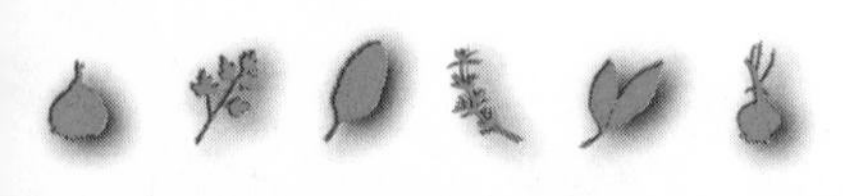

Strain the liquid into a saucepan and bring to a boil. When the sauce is reduced slightly (by about 1/4) whisk in the butter and mustard. Add the sun-dried tomatoes and chopped parsley. Pour sauce over short ribs and serve.

Serves 4

Ginger Marinated Beef Skewers with Spicy Peanut Dipping Saunce

Chris Cina, Executive Chef  **The Fourth Story Restaurant**

Marinade:

6	*Tbsp. each soy sauce and sesame oil*
2	*Tbsp. rice wine vinegar*
4	*Tbsp. grated fresh ginger*
2	*Tbsp. chopped garlic*
4	*lbs. top sirloin, thinly sliced and threaded onto skewers*

Combine marinade ingredients and spread evenly over beef. Marinate in refrigerator at least 2 hours. Remove from marinade and grill until done.

Spicy Peanut Dipping Sauce

2	*Tbsp. each olive and sesame oil*
1	*Tbsp. grated fresh ginger*
2	*Tbsp. each chopped garlic and crushed red chile flakes*
1	*bunch green onions, thinly sliced*
1	*lb. blanched unsalted peanuts*
1/4	*cup soy sauce*
1	*Tbsp. chopped cilantro*
	Salt and freshly ground black pepper to taste

Heat olive and sesame oils in a saucepan. Add ginger, garlic and green onions and cook, covered, over low heat for 30 seconds. Add the crushed red chiles and cook 30 seconds more (make sure heat is on very low as chile flakes can burn easily).

Add peanuts and soy sauce. Add just enough water to cover the peanuts. Bring to a boil and then reduce heat to a simmer for 30 minutes. Remove from heat and cool slightly. Purée in batches in a blender until smooth. Stir in chopped cilantro, and season with salt and pepper to taste.

Serves 16

Irish Beef Chili

Mary Clark **Bluepoint Bakery**

2 - 4	*Tbsp. olive oil*
2	*lbs. beef chuck, coarsely ground*
1	*lb. leanest parts pork shoulder, coarsely ground*
	Salt and freshly ground black pepper
1	*large onion, minced*
2	*ribs celery, cleaned and minced*
5	*cloves garlic, minced*
1/2	*cup tomato sauce*
2	*cups beef stock (may need 1/2 to 1 cup more)*
1 1/2	*Tbsp. ground cumin*
1	*Tbsp. dry oregano*
2 - 3	*Tbsp. ground New Mexico chiles*
2 - 3	*Tbsp. ground ancho or pasilla chiles*
1	*tsp. nutmeg*
2	*tsp. mace*
2	*tsp. sugar*
2	*Tbsp. unsweetened cocoa powder*
1/2	*bottle dark beer, or to taste*
6	*oz. Irish whisky, or to taste*
	For garnish: grated cheddar cheese, chopped white onion and fresh cilantro

Preheat oven to 225°. In a large Dutch oven, heat the oil over medium high heat. Season the meat with salt and pepper. Brown in the hot oil in very small batches, adding oil as necessary. Remove and set aside. Reduce heat and brown the onion, celery and garlic, adding a few drops of oil if it is too dry. Return the meat to the pot with any accumulated juices. Stir in the tomato sauce and stock, scraping any brown bits from the bottom. Mix the spices, sugar and cocoa powder in a small bowl and stir in a small amount of beer. Mix until there are no lumps and add this with the remaining beer to the chili. Bring mixture to a simmer; taste and season with additional salt and pepper if needed.

(continued)

Cover and place in the oven to cook at a very low simmer for 2 1/2 to 3 hours. Check after the first 30 minutes to make sure it is barely simmering. Check occasionally after that to see if it needs a little more liquid and to judge if it needs more chili powder or spices. During the last half hour, add the whisky.

When the meat is very tender the chili is done. Skim fat and taste; adjust the seasonings as needed. Serve with garnishes on the side.

Serves 8 to 10

Additional garnishes: sour cream, chopped jalapeño, chopped avocado, fried corn tortilla strips, chopped green onions and/or black beans.

T-Bone Fiorentina Style

Mary Clark **Bluepoint Bakery**

3 - 3 1/2	*lbs. T-bone steak, at least 3 inches thick*
1	*Tbsp. fresh rosemary, chopped*
1	*Tbsp. fresh sage, chopped*
1	*Tbsp. fresh thyme, chopped*
2	*Tbsp. freshly ground black pepper*
2	*Tbsp. salt*
1/4	*cup plus 2 Tbsp. very good extra-virgin olive oil*
6	*cloves garlic, sliced*
3	*lbs. spinach, stemmed, washed and dried*
	Juice of 1 lemon
	Salt and freshly ground black pepper

Remove T-bone from refrigerator at least 1 hour prior to grilling. Preheat gas grill or barbecue. The grill should be about 8 inches from the heat if using charcoal and a bit closer for gas. Be sure the grill surface is very hot before beginning to cook. You will need a very hot fire for about 20 minutes.

Rub herbs, pepper and salt into both sides of the steak and drizzle with 2 tablespoons olive oil. Place steak on hot grill and cook until well charred, about 12 to 15 minutes on the first side and another 10 minutes on the second side or until it is medium rare. Let rest off the heat for 10 to 15 minutes.

While steak is resting, heat 1/4 cup olive oil in a large skillet. When medium-hot, add garlic and sauté briefly. Increase heat and add spinach, tossing until just wilted. Season with lemon juice, salt and pepper.

Carve steak into slices. Arrange spinach and steak on 4 plates and serve.

Serves 4

Wasabe Marinated Flank Steak with Plum Wine Sauce

Christopher Rowe  **Barique**

1	*tsp. wasabe powder*
2	*Tbsp. soy sauce*
3	*Tbsp. olive oil*
2	*Tbsp. each minced garlic and minced shallots*
	Freshly ground black pepper
1	*flank steak*
	Jasmine rice, cooked

Mix wasabe powder and soy sauce to a smooth paste; blend in olive oil then add garlic, shallots and pepper to taste. Coat flank with mixture and marinate, covered, in refrigerator for at least 2 to 3 hours or overnight. Drain well and grill to desired doneness.

Plum Wine Sauce

1	*Tbsp. oriental sesame oil*
2	*cloves garlic, minced*
2	*shallots, minced*
1	*cup ripe plum slices*
	About 1/4 cup plum wine
1/2	*cup veal demi-glace*
	Additional plum slices

Heat sesame oil in a skillet. Add garlic and shallots, and sauté until lightly browned. Add plum slices and sauté briefly. Deglaze pan with plum wine. Add demi-glace and simmer until thickened. Strain sauce before serving over flank steak. Garnish with additional plum slices and serve with jasmine rice.

Serves 4

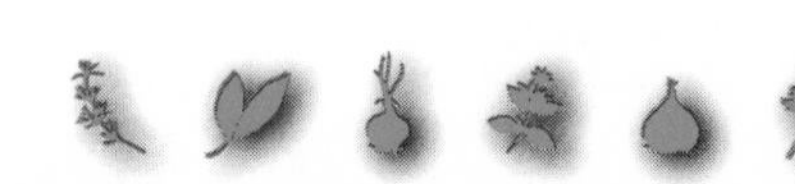

Veal Scaloppine with Artichokes

Ben Davis, Executive Chef  **Tony's Meats and Specialty Foods**

18	*small artichokes*
2	*lemons*
2	*shallots, peeled and chopped*
3	*cloves garlic, peeled and chopped*
2	*Roma tomatoes, cored and coarsely chopped*
1/2	*cup balsamic vinegar*
1/2	*cup red wine*
2	*sprigs rosemary*
2	*sprigs thyme*
1/4	*cup extra virgin olive oil*
	Salt and freshly ground black pepper to taste
	Chicken broth, preferably homemade

12	*slices veal top round, about 2 oz. each*
	Kosher salt and freshly ground black pepper
	Flour for dusting
1/4	*cup olive oil*
1/4	*cup butter, cut into chunks*
3	*Tbsp. chopped Italian parsley*

Preheat oven to 350°.

Using a sharp paring knife, remove about 2/3 of the heavy outer leaves from the artichokes, until just the tender inner leaves remain. Remove the stem and bottom of the leaves. Rub the artichokes all over with a cut lemon and place in cold water as you work.

In a large ovenproof pan, arrange drained artichokes with the stem side facing up. Scatter the shallots, garlic and tomatoes over, then add the vinegar and wine. Place the herbs on top and then add the olive oil; season with salt and pepper. Warm the chicken broth and add to the artichoke pan so that just the tops of the artichokes are above the liquid. Bring to a gentle boil on the stove. Cover with foil and bake in the oven

(continued)

until the artichokes are tender, about 25 to 35 minutes. Pierce the bottom with a knife point to check for doneness.

Remove the artichokes from the liquid; strain the liquid and reserve. Cut artichokes in half lengthwise and set aside.

Place the veal slices between 2 pieces of plastic wrap and pound gently until about 1/8 inch thick. Lightly season with salt and pepper. Dust with flour, shaking off the excess. Heat a heavy skillet and add 1/4 cup olive oil to the pan; immediately add the veal. Brown on both sides, then remove to a warm platter. Pour off excess oil; add the artichokes and heat through. Add 1 cup of the braising liquid and bring to a boil. Add the butter and swirl to combine. Season with salt and pepper.

Arrange the veal on 4 plates and pour sauce over the veal. Garnish with the chopped parsley.

Serves 4

A subtle wine is needed for this subtle dish, but one on the red side of the coin. Because this is an Italian recipe, an Italian wine works perfectly. Try a Barbera from the town of Alba in Piedmont. This grape at best is light, refreshing and has enough character to stand up to the tomatoes, garlic and wine without overpowering the dish. Pio Cesare makes a wonderful Barbera da Alba.

Asian Style Barbecued Pork Ribs

Andrea Alix, Owner and Executive Chef  **Cuisine Chez Vous**

Barbecue Sauce:

1	*Tbsp. garlic, minced*
1 1/2	*Tbsp. ginger, peeled and minced*
1/4	*cup green onions, chopped*
2	*Tbsp. sesame seeds, toasted*
1	*orange, zested and minced*
1/4	*cup hoisin sauce*
1/4	*cup plum sauce*
2	*Tbsp. oyster sauce*
2	*Tbsp. kecap manis (sweet soy)*
2	*Tbsp. honey*
2	*Tbsp. sesame oil*
1	*Tbsp. chili paste*
4	*slabs pork baby back ribs*

Preheat oven to 300°. Mix together all ingredients for Barbecue Sauce. Cut ribs into 3 sections and place in a shallow baking pan. Pour 1/2 of Barbecue Sauce over ribs. Let marinate in refrigerator for 1 hour.

Tightly cover ribs with foil and bake for 1 1/2 hours or until meat starts to separate from the bone. Remove from oven and cool slightly.

Coat ribs with more Barbecue Sauce, reserving some for basting. Preheat barbecue grill to high. Grill ribs for 2 to 3 minutes per side basting with remaining sauce. Remove from heat and serve immediately.

Serves 4 to 6

Falling-Off-the-Bone Pork Ribs

Cade Nagy, Executive Chef — **Paul's Catering**

1	*qt. water*
5	*cloves garlic*
1	*Tbsp. black peppercorns*
1	*bunch (6-8 sprigs) rosemary (any herb can be used)*
3	*whole racks of baby back ribs*
1	*cup Dry Rub (page 199)*
	Kansas City Barbecue Sauce (page 200)

Preheat oven to 200° or 150° if possible. Combine water, garlic, peppercorns and herbs in a large roasting pan.

Rub ribs with Dry Rub and place on a perforated pan that will fit over the water (do not let ribs touch the water). Cover with plastic wrap, then with aluminum foil. Bake for about 16 hours or until ribs are very tender.

Carefully remove ribs from pan. Brush ribs front and back with Barbecue Sauce. On a well-oiled grill, cook until sauce has baked into ribs, about 5 minutes on each side. Slice between bones and serve on a large platter.

Serves 4 to 6

Variation: Substitute beef ribs; cook no longer than 12 hours.

Green Chile Posole

Mary Clark **Bluepoint Bakery**

2	*Tbsp. cumin seeds*
2 1/2	*Tbsp. dry oregano*
30	*whole blanched almonds*
4	*Tbsp. sesame seeds*
2	*lbs. pork shoulder, cut in cubes (not too lean; marbling gives flavor)*
	New Mexico chili powder
	Salt and freshly ground black pepper
2	*Tbsp. olive oil*
2	*large onions, chopped*
3 - 5	*cloves garlic, minced*
1	*15-oz. can whole plum tomatoes, drained and crushed*
6 - 8	*Anaheim chilies (for milder chile) or 4 to 6 poblano chilies (for hot), roasted, skinned, seeded and chopped*
16	*oz. frozen posole*
4 - 6	*cups water or chicken stock*
3	*cups butternut squash, cut in 3/4 inch cubes*
1/2	*cauliflower, broken into small flowerets*
	Chopped cilantro, for garnish.

In a dry pan over medium high heat, toast the cumin and oregano, stirring constantly, until very aromatic, about 30 seconds. Remove and set aside to cool. Add almonds to pan and toast, stirring often. In the last few seconds add sesame seeds and continue to cook until seeds are lightly browned. Remove and cool. Grind cumin and oregano to a powder in a spice mill. Clean grinder, then grind almonds and sesame seeds to a fine paste.

Season pork generously with chili powder, salt and pepper. Heat oil in large Dutch oven. Brown pork in batches making sure not to crowd the pan. Remove and set aside. Drain excess fat, leaving about 1 tablespoon. Add onions to the pan and sauté until they have begun to soften. Add garlic, ground cumin and oregano; cook 1 more minute.

(continued)

Return pork to the pan and add tomatoes, chiles, posole and water. Cook at a low simmer until posole is half tender, about 45 to 60 minutes. Tate and adjust seasoning.

Add squash and cauliflower; cook approximately 45 more minutes, adding water as needed to keep a chile consistency. Be careful to not over-stir as the squash will break down. When posole, squash and cauliflower are tender, stir in almond-sesame paste. Taste and adjust seasoning with salt and pepper or chiles as desired. Serve with chopped cilantro garnish.

Serves 4 to 6

Pork Saté with Coconut-Lemongrass Dipping Sauce

Gigia Kolouch, Culinary Instructor  **The Natural Pantry**

Marinade:

1/2 onion, chopped
2 cloves garlic, peeled, smashed and chopped
1 Tbsp. palm or brown sugar
Juice of 1 lime
1 Tbsp. fish sauce
1 Tbsp. vegetable oil
1/2 tsp. tamarind pulp, dissolved into 2 Tbsp. water

1 lb. pork tenderloin, very thinly sliced and cut into strips 1/2 inch wide by 2 inches long
Wooden skewers

Marinade: Place all ingredients in a blender or food processor and purée until smooth. The sauce should be tangy, salty and sweet. Adjust seasonings to taste by adding sugar, lime or fish sauce.

Thread the meat strips like a ribbon onto wooden skewers and place in a shallow dish. Coat with marinade and let stand for 30 to 60 minutes, or marinate overnight in refrigerator.

Preheat broiler for at least 10 minutes. Remove the pork from the marinade and drain well. Broil for 3 to 4 minutes, turning once. You may also grill pork for a great flavor. Serve with Coconut-Lemongrass Dipping Sauce.

Serves 4

Coconut-Lemongrass Dipping Sauce

1/2	*cup crunchy peanut butter*
1	*onion, finely chopped*
1	*cup coconut milk*
1	*Tbsp. palm or brown sugar*
1	*tsp. cayenne pepper*
1	*stalk lemongrass, finely chopped*
1	*Tbsp. fish sauce*
1	*Tbsp. dark soy sauce*
	Juice of 1 lime

Mix ingredients together in a small saucepan, bring to a boil and keep warm.

Note: If you cannot find a jar of tamarind pulp, use a block of tamarind. Cut off a piece and soak it in hot water for 10 minutes. Strain to remove the seeds and fiber.

Jamaican Pork Tenderloin with Black Bean Salsa

Greg Barnhill, Executive Chef  **Three Tomatoes Catering**

Marinade:

1	*cup olive oil*
1	*Tbsp. cinnamon*
1	*Tbsp. nutmeg*
1	*Tbsp. ground allspice*
1	*tsp. ground cloves*
1	*tsp. crushed red pepper*
1/2	*cup raisins*
1/2	*cup lime juice*
1/2	*cup sugar*
1/2	*cup soy sauce*

2	*1 lb. pork tenderloins, cleaned and trimmed*

Place marinade ingredients in blender and blend until smooth. Marinate the pork for approximately 2 hours in refrigerator; turn occasionally.

Remove tenderloins from marinade (discard marinade). Grill for about 4 minutes on each side or until pork reaches an internal temperature of 145°. Serve with Black Bean Salsa on the side.

Serves 6

Black Bean Salsa

- 1 <u>each</u> *red, green and yellow pepper*
- 4 *jalapeños*
- 1 *medium red onion, diced*
- 4 *cups cooked black beans (if using canned, rinse and drain)*
- 1 *bunch cilantro, stems removed and chopped*
- 2 *Tbsp. cumin*
- 2 *Tbsp. lime juice*
- 6 *Tbsp. olive oil*
- *Salt and freshly ground black pepper to taste*

Seed and devein all peppers and dice. Combine with remaining ingredients. Season with salt and pepper and chill before serving.

Pork is a meat that can go with either red or white wine, depending on the preparation. The spices in this dish, along with the Black Bean Salsa, call for a red wine. Chateuneuf du Pape, a medium-bodied red wine from the Rhone Valley of France, would hold up well to the magnificent flavors.

Rosemary Pork Loin with Black Olive Tapenade

Conni Gallo, Chef  **Go Gourmet**

3	*Tbsp. fresh rosemary, minced*
2	*Tbsp. minced garlic*
1/2	*tsp. each salt and freshly ground black pepper*
1	*Tbsp. olive oil*
2	*pork tenderloins, trimmed*
	Fresh rosemary sprig for garnish

Preheat oven to 400°. In a mortar and pestle, make a coarse paste of the rosemary, garlic, salt and pepper. Spread over all sides of both pork loins with clean hands. Allow to stand at room temperature for 45 minutes.

Heat a large ovenproof sauté pan over moderately-high heat and add olive oil. Sear pork loins on all sides and transfer pan to oven. Roast 15 minutes for medium doneness. Remove from oven and cover pan with foil. Allow meat to rest 5 minutes before slicing.

Slice loins about 1/2 inch thick and serve with Black Olive Tapenade strewn across the slices. Garnish with a rosemary sprig.

Serves 4 to 6

Black Olive Tapenade

2	*cups Kalamata olives, pitted*
1	*2-oz. can anchovies with capers*
1	*small garlic clove, roughly chopped*
1/4	*cup best-quality olive oil*
	Freshly ground black pepper

In a food processor, place olives, anchovies and garlic. With the motor running, slowly add the oil until the tapenade is smooth; add an extra tablespoon of oil if necessary. Season with pepper to taste.

May be made up to 2 days in advance. Cover and refrigerate. Bring to room temperature before serving.

Makes 1 1/4 cups

This dish reflects Mediterranean countryside cuisine and what better choice than a good solid (and inexpensive) wine from that area. The P. Jaboulet Parallel 45 is a well-balanced and flavorful wine that will stand up well to the herbs and olives.

Whiskey and Cider Marinated Pork Tenderloin with Brandy Glazed Apples

Cade Nagy, Executive Chef  **Paul's Catering**

- *4 cups apple cider*
- *1 cup each brown sugar and whiskey*
- *6 pork tenderloins (6 to 7 oz. each), silverskin removed*

Combine apple cider, brown sugar and whiskey; mix well to dissolve sugar. Add pork. Cover and marinate, refrigerated, for at least 24 hours or up to 48 hours. Remove and drain well.

Grill on high heat to an internal temperature of 160°. Remove from heat and let rest for 5 to 10 minutes before slicing into 1 inch thick medallions. Place on a serving platter or on individual plates.

Brandy Glazed Apples

- *1/2 cup (1 stick) butter*
- *1/2 cup brown sugar*
- *6 Granny Smith apples, peeled, cored and sliced*
- *2 tsp. cinnamon*
- *1/2 cup brandy (cheap works just as well as expensive)*

Melt butter and brown sugar together in a large skillet over medium heat. Increase heat to high. Add apples and cinnamon; let cook until apples are soft, about 15 minutes.

Add brandy and ignite with a long kitchen match. Flame is blue - don't panic. Let flame burn out naturally. Spoon apples over pork medallions and serve.

Serves 6

Herb Encrusted Lamb Chops with Mint Mayonnaise

Cade Nagy, Executive Chef  **Paul's Catering**

Breading:

1/2	*bunch parsley, stems removed*
1/2	*bunch cilantro*
10	*basil leaves*
1	*cup dry breadcrumbs*

3	*whole lamb racks (about 7 to 8 bones per rack)*
1/2	*cup Dijon mustard*
2	*Tbsp. olive oil*

Breading: in food processor combine parsley, cilantro, basil and breadcrumbs. Process until herbs are finely chopped.

Slice racks into individual chops. Brush each chop lightly with mustard. Dip each chop into breading, coating well. Lightly coat each chop with olive oil and grill over high heat: about 2 minutes per side for rare, 7 to 10 minutes per side for well done.

Serves 6

Mint Mayonnaise

1	*cup mayonnaise*
1/4	*cup finely chopped mint leaves*
1	*tsp. lemon juice.*

Combine all ingredients and refrigerate for 1 hour before serving to blend flavors.

Yield: 1 1/4 cups

Lamb and Pinot Noir is one of the new classic food and wine pairings, especially with Colorado lamb. With the subtle flavors of red cherry and strawberry, and the typically silky finish of an aged Pinot Noir, there is no better pairing for the wonderful flavors of lamb. Try the Archery Summit from the red hills of Dundee, Oregon for the perfect match.

Lamb Rack Persillade

Conni Gallo, Chef  **Go Gourmet**

"This recipe will serve two people if using New Zeland lamb. If you are using the much larger American lamb, it may serve 3 to 4, although the portions will not be generous"

Marinade:

1	*cup olive oil*
1 1/2	*tsp. fresh rosemary, chopped*
1/4	*tsp. dried oregano leaves*
1/4	*tsp. freshly ground black pepper*
1/2	*cup lemon juice*
1/2	*cup dry vermouth*
1 1/2	*tsp. minced garlic*
1/3	*cup fresh mint, chopped*
1/2	*tsp. dried sage leaves*

1 *Lamb rack*

Persillade:

1	*cup parsley, chopped*
	Zest of 2 lemons, finely chopped
2	*garlic cloves, minced*
1	*tsp. olive oil*
	Salt and freshly ground black pepper, to taste

2	*Tbsp. clarified butter or oil*
	Dijon mustard

Cranberry and Dried Cherry Compote (page 196)

In a shallow glass container, combine Marinade ingredients. Add lamb rack and turn to coat completely; place in refrigerator for at least 1 hour.

Prepare Persillade by combining the parsley, lemon zest, garlic, olive oil, salt and pepper.

Heat oven to 400°. Remove lamb rack from marinade and pat dry. Heat an ovenproof sauté pan over moderately-high heat. Add butter and sear lamb rack, meat side down until golden brown. Turn and sear the other side. Transfer pan to the oven and roast to desired doneness.

Remove pan from oven and coat the lamb lightly with mustard, then with Persillade (meat side only). Turn oven to broil and place pan under heat to brown. Slice into chops. Serve with Cranberry and Dried Cherry Compote.

Serves 2-4

Roasted Lamb Sirloin with Polenta

John Mendes, Chef  **The Old Stone Church**

3	*cups each Chianti and beef stock*
6	*lamb sirloins*
	Salt and freshly ground black pepper
5	*Tbsp. olive oil*
1 1/2	*cups chopped celery*
1 1/2	*cups chopped carrots*
1 1/2	*cups chopped white onion*
3	*Roma tomatoes, cored and diced*

In a saucepan, combine Chianti and beef stock; simmer until reduced by 1/2. Preheat oven to 375°. Season lamb with salt and pepper.

In a hot skillet, sear lamb until well-browned on each side, about 2 to 3 minutes. Place in the oven and cook to medium rare, about 8 minutes. (Longer cooking will toughen the lamb.)

Heat oil in a large saucepan and sauté celery, carrots and onion until softened, stirring occasionally. Add tomatoes and chianti-beef reduction. Gently simmer until ready to serve.

Polenta

1	*cup milk*
1	*cup chicken stock*
2	*cups polenta*
6	*Tbsp. butter*
2	*sprigs rosemary, chopped*
1/2 – 1	*cup grated Parmesan cheese*
	Salt and freshly ground black pepper, to taste

Heat milk and chicken stock to a simmer, then slowly whisk in polenta. Cook slowly, stirring frequently, for about 15 to 18 minutes, then add butter and rosemary. Add Parmesan cheese a little at a time, stirring constantly, until desired thickness, creaminess and flavor is achieved. The polenta should be creamy, yet sturdy. Season to taste with salt and pepper.

Serve sauce over lamb with polenta on the side.

Serves 6

A Merlot will help balance and enhance the flavors of this robust dish. Look for the Canoe Ridge Merlot from Washington to bring depth and body to the meal.

Chicken and Poultry

Chicken and Poultry

BBQ Chicken

Cade Nagy, Executive Chef  **Paul's Catering**

2 whole chickens, cut into 8 pieces each
3 cups Kansas City Barbecue Sauce (page 200)
About 1/2 cup salad oil

In a large bowl, combine chicken pieces and Barbecue Sauce. Mix to coat each piece well.

Rub hot grill with a towel dipped in oil to season the grill well. Place chicken pieces on grill and cook just long enough to grill mark both sides. Remove and place on a baking sheet. Brush with remaining sauce. Cook in 350° oven until chicken reaches an internal temperature of 160°. Serve.

Serves 8 to 10

Chicken Yakitori

Wayne Conwell, Sushi Chef  **Restaurant Japon**

"Yakitori is grilled, skewered chicken. Most parts of the chicken, (thighs, leg, liver) can be used for yakitori, however since the thigh is most juicy, it is commonly preferred"

Soy sauce
Mirin (sweet cooking sake)
Sake (rice wine)
Sugar
2 lbs. chicken thighs, without bone or skin
1 bunch Japanese leeks or green onions
Wooden skewers, soaked in water for 30 minutes
Sesame seeds

Mix together 1 part each of soy sauce, mirin, sake and sugar; cook slowly until slightly thickened. Cut the chicken thighs into about 1 1/2 by 1 1/2 inch pieces. Put the chicken pieces into the prepared sauce and marinate for about 30 minutes in the refrigerator.

Cut the leek or green onions into pieces about 1 1/2 inches long. Skewer 3 to 4 pieces of chicken and onions on each skewer. Grill until chicken is cooked through. Sprinkle with sesame seeds and serve.

Serves 4 to 6

Note: Experimenting with pineapple juice, honey, chicken stock, or other liquids will improve the sauce. Unused sauce may be stored in refrigerator and used in a variety of grilled recipes.

Cuban Marinated Chicken Breast Stuffed with Herbed Goat Cheese

Greg Barnhill, Executive Chef  **Three Tomatoes Catering**

Marinade:

1/2	*cup each orange, lemon, lime and grapefruit juice*
1	*large garlic clove, peeled*
1	*shallot, peeled*
1/4 - 1/2	*Scotch Bonnet chile (to taste)*
1/2	*cup cilantro, chopped*
1	*tsp. freshly ground black pepper*
1	*cup olive oil*

Stuffing:

6	*oz. goat cheese*
1 1/2	*tsp. minced garlic*
2	*Tbsp. minced fresh basil*
2	*Tbsp. minced fresh oregano*
	Salt and freshly ground black pepper to taste
6	*chicken breasts, skin on*

Place all Marinade ingredients in blender and purée. In a small bowl, combine all Stuffing ingredients and mix well.

Loosen skin on chicken and stuff about 1 tablespoon of Stuffing mixture between skin and meat. Place in a shallow dish and pour Marinade over chicken, turning to coat well. Cover and marinate in refrigerator for about 1 hour. Remove from Marinade and drain well. Grill until done.

Serves 6

Grilled Rosemary Chicken Breasts

Gigia Kolouch, Culinary Instructor  **The Natural Pantry**

6	*boneless, skinless chicken breasts*
2	*Tbsp. fresh rosemary, chopped*
1/4	*cup olive oil*
	Juice of 1/2 lemon
1	*shallot, minced*
1	*Tbsp. Dijon mustard*
	Salt and freshly ground black pepper to taste

Rinse the chicken and pat it dry with a paper towel. Gently pound the chicken with a flat meat pounder until it is a uniform thickness. Mix the rosemary, olive oil, lemon, shallot, mustard, salt and pepper in a non-reactive shallow dish. Add the chicken and marinate in the refrigerator for 3 to 4 hours.

Grill the breasts over medium heat until they are browned and cooked all the way through, about 5 minutes to a side.

Serves 6

The herbs and Dijon mustard in this recipe almost beg for a crisp and dry white wine. One of the better pairings is an Italian Pinot Grigio produced by Ellena Walch.

Lemon-Herb Barbecued Chicken

Andrea Alix, Owner and Executive Chef  **Cuisine Chez Vous**

1 *whole chicken, cut into 8 pieces*

Marinade:

2 *lemons, zest and juice*
4 *cloves garlic, chopped*
2 *tsp. oregano, chopped*
2 *tsp. rosemary, chopped*
1 *Tbsp. thyme, chopped*
1 *tsp. chile flakes*
1 *Tbsp. Dijon mustard*
1 *Tbsp. honey*
1 *Tbsp. olive oil*
Kosher salt and freshly ground black pepper

Preheat oven to 350°. Place chicken pieces in a shallow baking pan. Mix together remaining ingredients for marinade and pour over chicken. Let marinate in refrigerator for 1 hour. Precook chicken in oven for 45 minutes before grilling.

Preheat grill to high. Finish cooking chicken on grill, basting with remaining marinade. Season to taste with kosher salt and freshly ground black pepper. Remove chicken to a platter and let rest for 3 to 5 minutes before serving.

Serves 4 to 6

Perfect Roast Chicken with Leek and Herb Sauce

Mary Clark  **Bluepoint Bakery**

1	*3 1/2 lb. natural chicken*
1	*Tbsp. butter*
	Salt and freshly ground black pepper to taste

Remove giblets and pat chicken dry. Rub with butter, salt and pepper inside and out. Let stand for 20 to 30 minutes to bring up to room temperature before roasting. Preheat oven to 375°.

Arrange a rack in a baking pan and put chicken on its side, thigh up, on the rack. Place chicken in oven and roast for 20 minutes. Remove chicken from oven and rotate so the other thigh is up, being careful to not tear the skin. Return to oven and roast for another 20 minutes.

Remove chicken from oven and rotate so the breast is up. Continue roasting for a final 20 minutes. Remove from the oven and place chicken (on the rack) over a large plate to catch the drippings. When chicken has rested for 15 to 30 minutes, carve and arrange on a large platter or individual plates.

Skim most of the fat off the pan drippings. (This fat may be used in place of butter to make a roux for thickening your sauce if desired.) The remaining drippings will be deglazed and incorporated into your sauce.

Serves 4

Leek and Herb Sauce

3	*Tbsp. butter*
1/4	*cup diced fennel*
1/3	*cup diced celery, including some leaves*
1/2	*cup leek, diced*
2	*shallots, diced*
2	*tsp. flour*
1/2	*cup white wine*
3	*Tbsp. minced fresh herbs (tarragon, chives, chervil and/or basil)*
2 1/2	*cups chicken stock*
	Salt and freshly ground white pepper

Heat butter in a saucepan over medium heat. Add fennel, celery, leek and shallots. Stir to coat with butter then cover and sweat until vegetables are transparent, approximately 4 minutes.

Remove cover and whisk in flour. Cook several minutes, stirring constantly, to make a roux. At the same time, deglaze the chicken roasting pan with wine. Add the deglazed pan juices, herbs and stock to the pan. Season with salt and pepper. Simmer until sauce has thickened and the flavor is intensified, about 5 to 8 minutes. Taste and adjust seasoning with salt and pepper.

Pan-Seared Duck Breasts with Merlot Reduction

Greg Barnhill, Executive Chef  **Three Tomatoes Catering**

6 *duck breasts, skin and fat removed*

Marinade:

2 *Tbsp. olive oil*
2 *Tbsp. soy sauce*
2 *tsp. minced garlic*
2 *tsp. minced shallots*
1 *Tbsp. chopped fresh rosemary*

Merlot Reduction:

4 *cups veal stock*
1 *cup Merlot*
2 *shallots, rough chop*
4 *sprigs fresh thyme*
2 *bay leaves*
6 *black peppercorns*
Salt and freshly ground black pepper to taste
Currant jelly, as needed

Marinade: whisk together all ingredients. Pour over duck breasts and marinate in refrigerator for 2 hours.

Merlot Reduction: combine veal stock, Merlot, shallots, thyme, bay leaves and peppercorns. Bring to a boil; reduce heat and simmer until reduced by 2/3. Season to taste with salt and pepper. Add a small amount of currant jelly as needed to balance flavors.

Drain duck breasts well and pan-sear to medium rare, about 2 minutes per side. Let rest for 5 minutes, then slice and arrange on a serving plate. Serve with Merlot Reduction.

Serves 6

Note: If desired, julienne duck skin and fry until crisp. Use to garnish duck breasts

Like lamb, duck and Pinot Noir is one of the new classical wine pairings. For this recipe, try one of the better offerings from California, the Pinot Noir from Talley down in the San Luis Obispo area. The concentrated red fruit and full-bodied finish make this a great choice.

Roast Turkey with Maple Gravy and Pear-Walnut Dressing

Chris Cina, Executive Chef  **The Fourth Story Restaurant and Bar**

1	*12 to 14 lb. fresh turkey*
5	*yellow onions, quartered*
8	*carrots*
8	*stalks celery*
12	*sprigs rosemary*
12	*cloves garlic*
1	*bunch parsley, rinsed*
2	*quarts (8 cups) red wine*
1	*cup maple syrup*
1/4	*cup olive oil*
2	*Tbsp. rosemary, chopped*
	Salt and freshly ground black pepper
1/2	*cup (1 stick) butter, room temperature*
1/2	*cup flour*
	Pear-Walnut Dressing (page 134)

Preheat oven to 325°. Place the onions, carrots, and celery in a roasting pan.

Stuff the rosemary sprigs, garlic cloves, and parsley into the cavity of the turkey. Place the turkey squarely in the roasting pan on top of the vegetables. Pour wine and maple syrup into the roasting pan. Rub the turkey with the olive oil and chopped rosemary. Season with salt and pepper. Roast for 3 to 3 1/2 hours, or to an internal temperature of 165°.

While the turkey is roasting, mix the butter and flour together until you have a paste. Store in refrigerator until needed.

When the turkey is done, remove from oven. Place the turkey on a platter and allow to rest for 20 to 30 minutes.

Strain the liquid from the roasting pan into a saucepan. Bring the liquid to a boil and whisk in the butter-flour mixture a little at a time until you have the desired consistency for gravy. Season with salt and pepper to your liking.

Serve turkey with gravy and Pear-Walnut Dressing.

Serves 8 to 10

The most commonly asked question around Thanksgiving is what wine goes with turkey? The full-bodied taste and slightly sweet spiciness of Gewurztraminer are a natural match. Look to Alsace in France for one of the better Gewurztraminers from Domaine Schlumberger.

Pear-Walnut Dressing

Chris Cina, Executive Chef  **The Fourth Story Restaurant and Bar**

1	*lb. bacon*
1/2	*white onion, diced*
2	*pears, peeled and diced*
1	*cup walnuts, toasted*
1	*Tbsp. garlic, chopped*
1	*Tbsp. thyme, chopped*
1	*Tbsp. parsley, chopped*
3	*quarts (12 cups) stale or toasted sourdough croutons, cut 1 by 1 inch*
3	*cups chicken stock*
	Salt and white pepper to taste

Preheat oven to 350°. Grease a 9 by 13 inch baking dish.

Sauté the bacon until well cooked. Add the onion, pears, walnuts, garlic, thyme and parsley. Cook covered, over low heat, until the onions become translucent. Add the bread cubes and mix well.

Add the chicken stock 1/2 cup at a time and stir well until all the stock has been incorporated. Season with salt and white pepper.

Spoon into prepared baking dish and bake for 20 to 30 minutes or until heated through.

Serves 8 to 10

Seafood

Dill

Seafood

Pancetta Wrapped Prawns

Greg Barnhill, Executive Chef  **_Three Tomatoes Catering_**

24 large shrimp, peeled and deveined
1 lb. pancetta, pre-sliced at the store into 24 thin slices
6 stainless steel skewers

Wrap each prawn with the pancetta and thread 4 prawns on each skewer. Grill for approximately 3 minutes per side over medium heat or until pancetta is crisp.

Serves 6

Skewered Shrimp and Pineapple

Conni Gallo, Chef  **Go Gourmet**

"Served on a bed of rice, this dish becomes elegant simplicity"

8 wooden skewers

1 lb. medium shrimp, peeled and deveined
1 fresh pineapple, peeled, cored, and cut into bite-size pieces
2/3 cup bottled teriyaki sauce

Place skewers in water to soak for 30 minutes prior to cooking.

In large shallow bowl, toss together shrimp, pineapple and teriyaki sauce. Cover and refrigerate for 1/2 hour.

Heat broiler or grill. Thread shrimp and pineapple onto skewers. Broil or grill until shrimp is pink and curled, 2 to 3 minutes on each side. Serve with rice, if desired.

Serves 4

Grilled shellfish served with fruit pairs well with the big buttery and oaky Chardonnays of the Central Coast of California. Try the Bernardus Chardonnay from Monterey for a perfect match.

Roasted Sea Bass with Molasses Baked Acorn Squash and Orange-Scented Rice Cake

Scott Elliott, Executive Chef  **Executive Tower Hotel**

Acorn Squash:

1 acorn squash
1 Tbsp. dark molasses
2 tsp. butter, melted

Rice Pancake:

2 eggs
1/2 cup milk
2 cups cooked white rice
3/4 cup Bisquick
1 Tbsp. orange juice
1 Tbsp. orange zest
1 Tbsp. diced red pepper
1 Tbsp. sliced green onions
1/4 cup canola oil, divided
Salt and freshly ground black pepper

4 6-oz. pieces of sea bass
1 Tbsp. canola or olive oil

Acorn Squash: Cut squash into 4 quarters and remove seeds. Bake in a 400° oven until tender when pierced with a fork. Combine molasses and butter; brush onto squash. Bake another 15 minutes. Keep warm.

Rice Pancake: Beat eggs with the milk. Add cooked rice, Bisquick, juice, zest, red pepper, green onions and 2 teaspoons of oil. Season with salt and pepper to taste. Heat remaining oil in a large skillet. Drop batter by tablespoons into heated skillet and cook pancakes until golden brown on each side. Remove and keep warm. Repeat with remaining batter, adding oil as needed.

(continued)

Sea Bass: Salt and pepper sea bass. In a very hot pan, add 1 tablespoon of oil, then sea bass. Cook until golden brown, turn and transfer to a baking sheet. Bake at 400° until done, approximately 8 minutes per inch of thickness.

Serves 4

Because of the complexity of this dish, you will need a wine that covers many flavor profiles. One of the most fun blends to come out of California recently is the Pine Ridge Chenin Blanc-Viognier blend. It combines the great acidity of the Chenin Blanc with the vibrant fruit of the Viognier, resulting in a wine that is an excellent match.

Cumin Dusted Wahoo

Greg Barnhill, Executive Chef  **_Three Tomatoes Catering_**

6 Tbsp. cumin seed
1 Tbsp. coriander seed
1 Tbsp. black peppercorns
1 Tbsp. kosher salt
6 7-oz. wahoo portions

In a coffee grinder, grind the cumin, coriander and peppercorns until medium-fine. Remove and mix with salt. Coat fish with the mixture and grill over medium heat for approximately 4 minutes per side.

Serves 6

Grilled Salmon with Thai-Coconut Vinaigrette

Carol Ann West  **Chef**

Marinade:

1	*lemongrass stalk, sliced into 1 inch pieces*
2	*Tbsp. soy sauce*
	Squeeze of lemon juice
1	*Tbsp. canola oil*
	Pinch dried cilantro
	Salt and freshly ground black pepper
1	*lb. salmon fillets, skinned and boned*

Vinaigrette:

1/4	*cup canola oil*
1	*Tbsp. sesame oil*
	Splash sherry
	Splash soy sauce
1/2	*tsp. grated fresh ginger*
1/2	*cup light coconut milk*
1/4	*cup rice vinegar*

1/2	*head napa cabbage, thinly sliced*
1	*pkg. rice stick noodles, soaked in hot water for 10 minutes, drained and cooled*
1	*cucumber, peeled, seeded and julienned*
2	*green onions, thinly sliced*
1	*carrot, peeled and julienned*
3	*radishes, thinly sliced*

Combine Marinade ingredients in a mixing bowl; add salmon and marinate in refrigerator for 1 hour. Drain Marinade and discard. Grill salmon on stove top, outdoor grill, or broil in the oven. Keep warm.

Combine Vinaigrette ingredients in a mixing bowl and mix well. Arrange cabbage on a serving platter. Arrange rice noodles on top of cabbage, then garnish attractively with remaining vegetables. Place grilled salmon on top and drizzle with Vinaigrette.

Serves 4 to 6

Pan-Seared Salmon with Bourbon Glaze and Fresh Raspberries

Jill Richter, Chef — ***Jax Fish House***

1	*cup bourbon*
1	*cup honey*
4	*6-oz. salmon fillets*
	Salt and freshly ground black pepper to taste
1	*Tbsp. cumin*
1	*pint fresh raspberries, washed*

Mix bourbon and honey together.

Sprinkle salmon fillets with salt, pepper and cumin. Place top side down in a hot sauté pan. Cook for 2 to 3 minutes. Turn over and drizzle with bourbon glaze; add raspberries to pan. Cook another 2 to 3 minutes or until done to your liking. Carefully lift the salmon out of the pan with a spatula; pour glaze and berries over fish.

Serves 4

Salmon Fillets with Caponattina

Scott Elliott, Executive Chef  **Executive Tower Hotel**

Caponattina:

3	*Tbsp. olive oil*
1	*medium eggplant, peeled, large dice*
1	*yellow onion, roughly chopped*
1	*summer squash, large dice*
2	*ripe tomatoes, squeezed and chopped*
2	*Tbsp. minced garlic*
1/2	*tsp. minced fresh rosemary*
1/2	*tsp. fresh thyme*
2	*Tbsp. sugar*
1/4	*cup sherry vinegar*
	Salt and freshly ground black pepper
4	*6-oz. salmon fillets, grilled*

Heat olive oil in a large skillet. Sauté eggplant, onion and squash for about 5 minutes. Add tomato, garlic and herbs. Simmer another 5 minutes. Add sugar and sherry vinegar; simmer for 20 minutes, stirring occasionally. Season with salt and pepper. Serve immediately with grilled salmon.

Serves 4

Salmon Steaks with Yakaniku Sauce

Scott Elliott, Executive Chef  **Executive Tower Hotel**

Sauce:

1	*Tbsp. sesame seeds*
1/4	*cup soy sauce*
1/2	*cup mirin*
1/4	*cup sake*
1/4	*cup low-sodium chicken stock*
1/2	*Tbsp. minced ginger*
1	*tsp. minced garlic*
	Pinch red chili flakes or to taste
4	*6-oz. salmon steaks*

Sauce: Place sesame seeds in a small saucepan over low heat. Toast, stirring occasionally, until golden brown. Watch carefully as they burn easily. Add remaining sauce ingredients and simmer for 30 minutes.

Grill or broil salmon until done. Serve with Yakaniku Sauce and Pineapple-Ginger Rice (page 170).

Serves 4

Wok Smoked Salmon

Gigia Kolouch, Culinary Instructor  **The Natural Pantry**

1 1/2 lbs. salmon fillet, skin on

for the marinade:

- 1 Tbsp. fresh lemon or lime juice
- 1/4 cup dry white wine or sherry
- 3 Tbsp. light or thin soy sauce
- 1 Tbsp. sugar
- 1 Tbsp. kosher or sea salt
- 2 green onions, smashed
- 4 thin slices of ginger, smashed
- 1 tsp. five spice powder

for the wok:

- 1/3 cup dry tea leaves, such as oolong, lapsang soochong or Earl Grey
- 1/3 cup white rice (raw)
- 1/3 cup packed brown sugar
- 1 Tbsp. Szechwan peppercorns, crushed
- 1 cinnamon stick, crushed
- 3 large pieces fresh or dried tangerine peel
- 4 pieces star anise, crushed

for the garnish:

- 1 1/2 tsp. sesame oil
- 1 tsp. black sesame seeds
- 1/4 cup cilantro leaves

Remove the scales from the skin and debone fish, if necessary. Place the fish, flesh side down, in a shallow baking dish. Combine the marinade ingredients and pour over the fish. Marinate in the refrigerator for at least 2 hours or as long as overnight.

(continued)

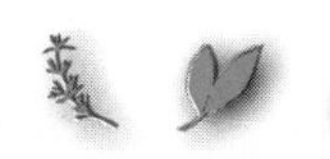

You will need a small metal rack or steamer that can fit in your wok. Remove the salmon from the marinade and place it on the rack in the steamer. Add 1 to 2 inches of water to the bottom of your wok. Cover tightly and steam at high heat for 6 to 8 minutes, until it is just cooked. Set aside the salmon, leaving it on the rack. Drain the water from the wok. This part of the recipe may be done several hours ahead of time.

Line the bowl and the lid of the wok with 3 layers of aluminum foil, making sure there are 3 to 4 inches hanging over the edge of the wok. Combine the tea, rice, sugar, peppercorns, cinnamon, tangerine peel and star anise. Sprinkle it in the bottom of the wok.

Place the fish on its rack over the tea mixture. Turn the heat to high. In 4 to 6 minutes, you should see some smoke rising from the wok. Cover the wok and crimp the foil together, leaving 1 to 2 inches open. This gap will allow you to make sure the smoke is still working. Leave the wok on high for 10 minutes, maintaining a steady, thin stream of smoke. If you get a large amount of smoke, turn down the wok, or tighten the opening. Turn off the heat and let the fish stand for 5 minutes to cool before opening.

Take the wok outside to a well-ventilated area. Remove the lid and foil. The fish should be a nice golden brown. If the fish is not smoked enough, you may add some more brown sugar, reseal the wok and return it to high heat.

After the fish is done, discard the foil outside, to minimize smoke in your kitchen. Remove the fish to a serving platter and drizzle it with sesame oil. Sprinkle the black sesame seeds and cilantro leaves over the salmon and serve hot or room temperature.

Serves 4 to 6

Herbed Crusted Swordfish

Greg Barnhill, Executive Chef  **Three Tomatoes Catering**

1 bunch fresh basil
2 sprigs fresh rosemary
1 bunch fresh oregano
1 bunch fresh sage
1 baguette, cut into 2 inch pieces
6 7-oz. swordfish steaks
1 cup melted butter
Salt and freshly ground black pepper to taste

Remove stems from herbs. Place herbs in a food processor along with the bread pieces and pulse until bread is in crumbs and herbs are incorporated. Spread herb mixture onto a flat plate or pan.

Dip the swordfish into the melted butter and then into the herbed breadcrumbs to coat both sides evenly. Grill over low heat (so breadcrumbs do not burn) for approximately 4 minutes per side or until the fish is medium.

Serves 6

Grilled Tuna Over Potato Salad Provençal

Jill Richter, Chef — **Jax Fish House**

Potato Salad:

3	*lbs. new potatoes, boiled, cooled and diced*
1/2	*lb. haricot vert, blanched*
2	*hard boiled eggs, diced*
1/2	*cup niçoise olives*
1/2	*cup capers, drained*

Dressing:

1/4	*cup lemon juice or to taste*
1/2	*cup olive oil or to taste*
1	*tsp. salt*
1	*Tbsp. freshly ground black pepper*
3	*Tbsp. fresh thyme, chopped*

4	*6-oz. pieces of yellowfin tuna*
	Salt and freshly ground black pepper

Potato Salad: In a large bowl, combine potatoes, haricot vert, eggs, olives and capers.

Dressing: In a small bowl, whisk together lemon juice, olive oil, salt, pepper and thyme. Pour over potato mixture and combine gently, but thoroughly. May be served chilled or at room temperature.

Season tuna with salt and pepper. Grill to desired degree of doneness. Serve on top of potato salad.

Serves 4

Pepper-Crusted Yellowfin Tuna

Greg Barnhill, Executive Chef  ***Three Tomatoes Catering***

- 1 *Tbsp. black peppercorns*
- 1 *Tbsp. white peppercorns*
- 1 *Tbsp. pink peppercorns*
- 2 *Tbsp. coriander seeds*
- 2 *Tbsp. kosher salt*
- 6 *7-oz. yellowfin tuna steaks*
- 1 *cup melted butter*

In a coffee grinder, grind all peppercorns and coriander seeds until medium-fine. Mix with the salt and spread onto a flat plate or pan.

Dip tuna steaks in the melted butter and then in the peppercorn mixture to coat. Grill on medium heat for 4 minutes per side or until medium rare.

Serves 6

Tuna is as much a red meat as steak and veal, especially Ahi and Yellowfin. To bring out the flavors without overpowering this dish (a hard task with all of the spiciness from the peppercorns) try a good Australian Shiraz that is on the lighter side. Rosemount Estates produces great Shiraz all across the price spectrum, and their regular bottling will make a perfect match.

Pasta and Grains

Pasta and Grains

Bow Tie Pasta with Blackened Chicken, Roasted Corn and Vodka Cream Sauce

Greg Barnhill, Executive Chef  **Three Tomatoes Catering**

- 1 *lb. bow tie pasta*
- 1 *lb. boneless, skinless chicken breasts*
- 4 *Tbsp. Paul Prudhomme blackening spices*
- 4 *cups frozen (thawed) or fresh corn kernels*
- 1 *Tbsp. olive oil*
- 1/2 *cup vodka*
- 1 1/2 *cups spaghetti sauce (your favorite brand)*
- 4 *cups heavy cream*
- 1 *bunch basil leaves, julienned*
- *Salt and freshly ground black pepper*

Cook pasta according to package directions; drain well and keep warm.

Coat chicken with blackening spices and grill until done. Slice into strips and keep warm. Spread corn on a baking sheet and roast at 425° until browned, about 5 minutes.

In a large skillet, heat olive oil and sauté the chicken strips and corn for 1 minute. Deglaze the pan with vodka. Add spaghetti sauce and mix well. Add cream and reduce until thick, about 5 minutes. Stir in the cooked pasta and basil. Season to taste with salt and pepper. Serve.

Serves 6

A German Riesling helps cut through the cream and spice in this dish. With its moderate alcohol and off-dry palate, the spiciness and acidity of a Spatlese quality from Kloster Eberbach is a good choice.

Creamy Baked Ziti

Conni Gallo, Chef  **Go Gourmet**

3	*Tbsp. olive oil, divided*
3	*large yellow bell peppers, chopped*
1	*large onion, chopped*
3	*garlic cloves, minced*
1 1/2	*cups heavy cream*
	Salt and freshly ground black pepper to taste
1 1/2	*lbs. mushrooms, thinly sliced*
4	*medium red bell peppers, julienned*
1	*lb. ziti*
8	*green onions, green part only, thinly sliced on the diagonal*
2	*cups freshly grated Parmesan cheese*

Preheat oven to 375°.

In a large saucepan, heat 1 Tbsp. of the oil. Add yellow peppers, onion and garlic; cover and cook over moderately-low heat for about 30 minutes, stirring occasionally. Stir in cream. In batches, pour mixture into blender and purée. Transfer to a large bowl and season with salt and pepper.

Meanwhile, in a large saucepan, heat remaining oil. Add mushrooms and red bell peppers. Sauté until mushrooms release and reabsorb their liquid, about 8 minutes. Season with salt and pepper.

Fill a 6 to 7-quart pot 3/4 full of salted water; bring to a boil. Stir ziti into the boiling water and cook until just tender, about 10 minutes. Drain ziti, reserving 1 cup of the pasta water. In the large bowl containing the yellow pepper sauce, stir in reserved cooking water, ziti, mushroom mixture, scallion greens and 1 1/2 cups Parmesan. Season with salt and pepper. Transfer mixture to a shallow baking dish and sprinkle with remaining Parmesan.

Bake until hot and pasta begins to brown, 20 to 25 minutes.

Serves 8 to 10

Fettuccine Jambalaya

Greg Barnhill, Executive Chef  **_Three Tomatoes Catering_**

1	*lb. fettuccine*
1	*lb. jumbo shrimp (about 18), shelled and deveined*
4	*Tbsp. olive oil*
12	*oz. tasso ham, diced*
6	*cups spaghetti sauce (homemade or from a jar)*
4	*cups water-packed artichoke hearts, drained and cut in half*
10	*Tbsp. butter, cold*
1/2	*bunch fresh basil leaves, julienned*
	Salt and freshly ground black pepper to taste
	Fresh basil sprigs

Cook fettuccine in boiling water according to package directions. Drain well and keep warm.

Sauté shrimp in olive oil for 2 minutes. Add the tasso and sauté for 2 minutes more. Add spaghetti sauce, artichoke hearts and butter. Cook until butter is melted into the sauce. Mix in the cooked fettuccine and basil. Season to taste with salt and pepper. Toss and remove shrimp. Place the pasta mixture on plates and garnish with the shrimp and fresh basil sprigs.

Serves 6 to 8

Thom Wise's World Famous Lasagna

Thom Wise  **Former Restaurant Critic - Rocky Mountain News**

Meat mixture:

1 1/2	*lbs. spicy Italian sausage, bulk*
4 - 5	*cloves garlic, whole (stick a toothpick through cloves)*
1/4	*cup fresh basil, chiffonade*
1	*28-oz. can Progresso tomatoes with basil (or equivalent of fresh tomatoes) seeded and coarsely chopped)*
2	*6-oz. cans tomato paste*

Cheese mixture:

2	*eggs*
3	*cups ricotta cheese*
1	*cup grated Parmesan cheese*
1	*bunch coarsely chopped Italian parsley*
	Salt and freshly ground black pepper to taste

1	*bunch spinach*
	Olive oil
1	*16-oz. box lasagna noodles*
1	*lb. mozzarella cheese, grated*

Preheat oven to 350°. Brown sausage with garlic cloves; drain off any fat, then add all other ingredients. Simmer at least 1 hour so everyone gets to know one another and the mix is fairly dry. Remove garlic cloves.

Next, prepare cheese mixture by combining all ingredients. Refrigerate.

Clean and stem spinach. Sauté in small batches in a small amount of olive oil (just enough to coat bottom of sauté pan). Drain on paper towels. Cook lasagna noodles as per directions on box. Drain.

To assemble: in an oblong (9 by 13 inch) lasagna pan, layer 1/2 of the noodles, then 1/2 of the cheese mixture, then 1/2 of the spinach, 1/2 of the mozzarella and finally 1/2 of the meat mixture. Repeat. Bake at 350° for 30 minutes. Let rest for 5 minutes before serving.

Serves 8

The generally high acidity and rich flavors of the Sangiovese grape from Chianti will make a great pairing with the robust flavors of this Lasagna. Look for the Riserva from Dievole.

Orzo with Wild Mushrooms

Amy Hoyt, Owner  **Heavenly Baking and Catering**

1/2	*onion, finely chopped*
2	*cloves garlic, minced*
4	*Tbsp. butter, divided*
10	*porcini or crimini mushrooms, thinly sliced*
1/4	*cup red wine*
1/4	*lb. (4 oz.) orzo pasta*
1/4	*cup shredded Parmesan cheese*
	Salt and freshly ground black pepper to taste

Sauté the onion and garlic in 2 tablespoons of the butter until transparent. Add the mushrooms and cook until softened. Add wine and remaining 2 tablespoons butter; cook until slightly thickened.

Meanwhile, cook the pasta in boiling salted water according to package directions. Drain well. Pour sauce over the hot orzo and sprinkle with Parmesan; stir gently. Season to taste with salt and pepper.

Serves 4

Pasta all' Genovese

Ben Davis, Executive Chef  **Tony's Meats and Specialty Foods**

6	*cloves garlic, peeled*
1/4	*cup pine nuts*
4	*cups basil leaves*
24	*mint leaves*
1/2 - 1	*cup extra-virgin olive oil*
6	*small Yukon Gold potatoes*
1	*cup baby green beans, cut into 1inch lengths*
1	*lb. high quality dried pasta—use penne, fusilli, radiatore or other cut no more than 3 inches in length*
	Freshly grated Parmesan-Reggiano cheese to taste

In a food processor, purée the garlic, pine nuts, basil and mint with the olive oil to a medium-coarse purée.

Boil the potatoes until just soft. Drain; cool and peel. Cut into chunks and set aside. Blanch the green beans in boiling salted water for 1 minute, then plunge into ice water. Drain and set aside.

Cook the pasta in boiling salted water until slightly underdone. Drain, reserving the water. In another pan large enough to hold all the ingredients, bring about 1/2 of the reserved pasta water to a boil. Add half of the pesto and return to a boil. Then add the potatoes and the pasta. Heat through, adding more water if necessary to create a sauce-like consistency. When the pasta is hot, add the green beans and heat through. Add more water as needed; pasta should not be dry. Add additional pesto to taste.

When all the ingredients are hot, remove from the heat, toss in some Parmesan cheese and stir to combine. Divide between four bowls and pass extra Parmesan cheese.

Serves 4

Smoked Chicken Penne Pasta with Stone Ground Mustard

Greg Barnhill, Executive Chef  **Three Tomatoes Catering**

1 lb. red peppers
1 lb. mushrooms, sliced
4 Tbsp. minced garlic
2 lbs. grilled or smoked chicken breast, cut into strips
Olive oil
6 cups heavy cream
6 Tbsp. stone ground mustard
1 lb. baby spinach
2 lbs. penne pasta, cooked al dente
Salt and freshly ground black pepper to taste

Preheat oven to 450°. Place red peppers on a baking sheet lined with foil. Roast for 30 to 45 minutes, turning often, or until black and charred all over. Place in a paper or plastic bag, close tightly (or in a bowl covered with plastic wrap) and let stand for about 10 minutes. Pull out core, remove seeds and peel off skin. Julienne.

In a large pan, sauté the mushrooms, garlic and chicken breast in olive oil until caramelized. Add the cream and reduce until thick, about 5 minutes. Mix in the mustard, spinach and red peppers. Add the cooked pasta and toss until well-coated and heated through. Season with salt and pepper. Serve.

Serves 6 to 8

This dish requires a good California Chardonnay that is not sweet, has high acidity and is completely dry to cut through the richness of the sauce. Grgich Hills Chardonnay from Napa Valley is a good pick.

Tortellini with Prosciutto, Mushrooms and Peas

Greg Barnhill, Executive Chef  **Three Tomatoes Catering**

2 lbs. ricotta cheese-filled tortellini
4 Tbsp. olive oil
4 cups sliced mushrooms (your choice)
4 Tbsp. minced garlic
1 lb. prosciutto, julienned
6 cups heavy cream
2 cups shredded Parmesan cheese
4 Tbsp. butter
1 16-oz. bag frozen peas, thawed
Salt and freshly ground white pepper to taste

Cook tortellini according to package directions; drain well and keep warm.

In a large skillet, heat olive oil and sauté mushrooms until caramelized (browned). Add the garlic and prosciutto; sauté until garlic begins to brown. Add cream and cook over medium heat until reduced by 1/3. Add Parmesan cheese, butter and peas. Season to taste with salt and pepper. Add cooked tortellini; toss and serve.

Serves 6

This full-flavored dish needs a full-flavored Italian wine that is a bit on the sweet side. Amarone della Valpolicella is made by first drying out the grapes to concentrate flavors before making the wine. One of the better and most accessible producers is Tommasi.

Tuscan Style Pasta with Tuna, Capers and Olives

Greg Barnhill, Executive Chef  **Three Tomatoes Catering**

2 lbs. radiatore pasta
3 lbs. fresh yellowfin tuna
4 Tbsp. minced garlic
4 Tbsp. capers, drained
4 Tbsp. chopped Kalamata olives
Olive oil
6 tomatoes, peeled, seeded and chopped
1 cup white wine
6 Tbsp. chiffonade of basil (thin strips)
6 Tbsp. Clam Butter (see next page)
3 Tbsp. raisins

Cook pasta according to package directions. Drain and rinse with cold water; drain again. Grill tuna to rare and cut into bite-size pieces.

In a large skillet, sauté the garlic, capers and olives in olive oil for 30 seconds. Add the tomatoes, white wine, basil and tuna. Add the Clam Butter and stir until well blended. Mix in cooked pasta. Cook over low heat until heated through. Season to taste with salt and pepper. Stir in raisins and serve.

Serves 8

Clam Butter

1	*lb. (4 sticks) unsalted butter, softened*
4	*Tbsp. clam base*
2	*Tbsp. fresh lemon juice*
2	*tsp. Tabasco*
2	*tsp. Worcestershire*
1	*Tbsp. minced garlic*
1	*Tbsp. minced shallots*
1	*bunch parsley, stemmed and chopped*

With an electric mixer, combine all ingredients until well blended. Store in refrigerator.

Citrus Basmati Rice

Gigia Kolouch, Culinary Instructor  **The Natural Pantry**

2	*cups basmati or long grain rice*
2	*Tbsp. olive oil*
1	*medium sized onion, peeled, cut in half lengthwise, then sliced into paper-thin rings*
1	*clove garlic, peeled and minced*
1/2	*tsp. minced fresh hot green chile or 1/8 tsp. cayenne pepper*
1	*tsp. each lemon zest and orange zest*
1	*tsp. salt*
3	*cups chicken stock or water, heated*
2	*Tbsp. toasted pine nuts*
1/4	*cup chopped fresh mint*

Rinse rice in a bowl until water is clear. Cover with more water and let soak while you prepare the rest of the ingredients. Drain rice in a strainer when you are ready. Preheat oven to 325°.

The rice dish cooks on top of the stove and in the oven, so use a heavy, flame and ovenproof, 2-quart sauté pan. Heat the oil over medium heat. Add the onion, garlic, green chile and zest. Sauté for 2 to 3 minutes or until onions turn brown at the edges. Add the drained rice and salt. Turn the heat to medium-low. Sauté the rice for 7 to 8 minutes, stirring frequently, or until the rice is translucent and well coated with the oil.

Add the heated stock. Keep stirring and cooking on a medium low flame for another 5 to 6 minutes. When the top of the rice begins to look dry (there will still be a little liquid left at the bottom of the pot), cover with a tight-fitting lid and place in the oven for 20 to 25 minutes or until rice is cooked through. Remove from the oven and let stand, covered, in a warm place for 10 minutes. (If kept covered and in a warm place, this rice will stay warm for a good half hour.) Garnish with pine nuts and mint before serving.

Serves 6 to 8

Havana Rice

Dan Barnes, Executive Chef  **Denver Buffalo Company**

"Here is a simple recipe—full of flavor—to use up leftover rice!"

2	*Tbsp. olive oil*
2	*Tbsp. butter*
2	*Tbsp. minced garlic*
1/2	*cup diced onion*
1/2	*cup diced ham*
1	*cup tomato sauce*
1	*bay leaf*
1	*tsp. dried oregano*
3	*cups warm cooked white rice*
	Fresh cilantro sprigs for garnish

Heat a large skillet and add olive oil. When oil becomes fragrant and hot, add butter and blend together. Add garlic and onion; cook until onion is translucent. Add ham, tomato sauce, bay leaf and oregano. Simmer 5 to 10 minutes. Remove bay leaf and add rice. Mix well and serve garnished with fresh cilantro.

Serves 6

Holiday Wild Rice Pilaf

Conni Gallo, Chef  **Go Gourmet**

"If serving beef, such as prime rib or tenderloin, use beef or veal stock. If your holiday means roasting a turkey or a ham, chicken stock would be appropriate. When in doubt, vegetable stock is always delicious"

1	*cup wild rice*
4	*cups chicken, beef or vegetable stock*
1	*Tbsp. butter*
1	*cup chopped celery*
1	*cup chopped onion*
3/4	*cup long-grain white rice*
1/2	*cup dry sherry*
1/2	*tsp. dried sage, crushed*
1/2	*cup roughly chopped walnuts*
	Salt and freshly ground black pepper, to taste

In a large saucepan, combine wild rice and stock. Cover and bring to a boil; reduce heat and simmer for 40 minutes. Set aside. Preheat oven to 350°.

Melt butter in a large sauté pan. Add celery and onion; sauté until translucent. Add white rice and stir to coat each grain of rice. Add wild rice with liquid, sherry and sage; stir just to combine. Cover and bring to a boil. Transfer to oven for 20 minutes.

When rice is tender, stir in walnuts. Season with salt and pepper. Serve immediately.

Serves 8

Onion and Porcini Mushroom Rice Pilaf

Conni Gallo, Chef  **Go Gourmet**

1/2	*cup dried porcini mushrooms, rinsed of any dirt*
1	*Tbsp. butter*
2	*Tbsp. diced onion*
1	*cup long-grain rice, preferably jasmine*
2	*cups hot chicken stock*
	Salt and freshly ground black pepper, to taste

Preheat oven to 350°. In small saucepan, cover porcini mushrooms with water and bring to a boil. Turn heat off and allow the mushrooms to soften in the hot water at least 30 minutes. Drain and chop; set aside.

In an ovenproof saucepan or a sauté pan with lid, melt butter over medium heat. Add onion and cover; cook over low heat for 5 minutes. Add rice and stir to coat grains. Add hot stock, mushrooms, salt and pepper. Cover and bring to a boil. Transfer covered pan to oven for 20 minutes. Serve immediately.

Serves 4

Pineapple Ginger Rice

Scott Elliott, Executive Chef  **Executive Tower Hotel**

1	*Tbsp. butter*
2	*Tbsp. minced ginger*
1	*Tbsp. minced garlic*
1/4	*cup finely diced red bell pepper*
1/4	*cup fresh pineapple, medium dice*
1/4	*cup chopped green onions*
4	*cups cooked rice*
1/2	*cup pineapple juice*
	Salt and freshly ground black pepper to taste

Heat butter in a large skillet. Sauté ginger, garlic and red pepper until garlic is opaque. Add pineapple, green onions and cooked rice. Cook until warmed through, then add pineapple juice. Cook until liquid has evaporated. Season with salt and pepper.

Serves 6 to 8

Risotto with Caramelized Onions and Pancetta

Ben Davis, Executive Chef  **Tony's Meats and Specialty Food**

2 yellow onions
2 oz. pancetta
1/2 cup butter
6 cups water
1 cup chicken broth, preferably homemade
1 Tbsp. olive oil
1 cup Arborio or carneloni rice
1/2 cup grated Parmesan-Reggiano cheese
Kosher salt
1/2 Tbsp. fresh thyme leaves
Extra virgin olive oil

Peel, halve and slice the onions into thin strips. Dice the pancetta; set aside.

In a heavy skillet, heat 1/2 cup butter until it foams. Add the onions and reduce the heat to medium. Cook, stirring often, until the onions are dark brown and sweet, about 20 to 30 minutes. Pour off any excess butter and set aside.

Combine the water and stock in a saucepan and bring to a boil.

In a large wide pan, heat the olive oil. Add the pancetta and cook until it is firm but not crisp. Add the rice and stir to combine. Add enough of the water and stock mixture to just cover the rice. STIR WITH A WOODEN SPOON!!! Continue stirring and add more liquid when the rice on the top becomes exposed. After the second addition of broth, add some Parmesan cheese, a pinch of salt and the thyme leaves. Continue stirring.

After stirring for about 12 to 15 minutes, add the caramelized onions. Stir and add the broth until the rice is firm, but does not stick in your teeth. Add more cheese and season with salt if desired.

Remove from the heat and let rest for 2 minutes. Pour into serving bowls, drizzle with olive oil and serve immediately. Pass extra cheese on the side.

Serves 4

Sipping wine with risotto echoes the flavors of all the ingredients used in its preparation. Look for a lighter style red such as Rosso di Montalcino from Tuscany. Avignonesi is one of the better producers in this area.

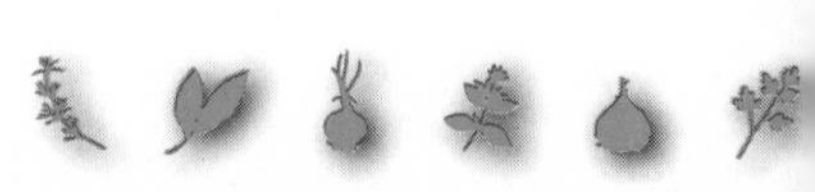

Grilled Polenta with Poblano Peppers

Cade Nagy, Executive Chef  **Paul's Catering**

5	*poblano peppers*
4	*cups chicken stock*
1/2	*cup heavy cream*
1	*lb. cornmeal*
1/2	*cup grated Parmesan cheese*
	Cooking spray

Place peppers directly over an open flame and roast until skin blackens. Turn and continue roasting until blackened all over. Place in a bowl and cover with plastic wrap; let stand about 30 minutes. Remove seeds and peel.

Purée peppers in a food processor. Place in a large saucepan with chicken stock and cream. Bring to a boil. Slowly pour in cornmeal, stirring constantly, until smooth, thick and creamy. Remove from heat and stir in cheese. Pour into a greased 9 by 13 inch casserole dish. Cover and refrigerate until firm. Cut into triangles about 3 inches in size.

Spray polenta triangles with cooking spray and grill until hot, turning once. Transfer to a platter and serve. These can also be deep fried, baked, broiled or the polenta can be served from the creamy stage before chilling.

Serves 8

Variation: Cut chilled polenta into 1 inch squares and wrap with a strip of prosciutto. Serve on a skewer as a great bite-size appetizer. Best served at room temperature.

Butternut Squash Stuffing

Mary Clark **Bluepoint Bakery**

4	*cups toasted bread cubes*
1/3	*cup hazelnuts, toasted, skinned and chopped*
1 1/3	*cups butternut squash, cubed*
3	*oz. pancetta, sliced thin and chopped*
1	*cup onions, chopped*
10	*oz. (1 stick plus 2 Tbsp.) unsalted butter*
2/3	*cup fresh sage leaves*
1 1/2	*cups chicken stock to moisten (more as needed)*
	Salt and freshly ground black pepper to taste

Preheat oven to 375°. Combine bread and hazelnuts in a large mixing bowl. Cook squash cubes in boiling salted water to just blanch, 1 to 2 minutes. Drain well and add to bread mixture.

Cook pancetta over medium heat in a large sauté pan until fat is rendered. Add onions and sauté briefly. Scrape pancetta, onions and any remaining fat into the bread mixture. Heat butter in the same sauté pan over high heat until it starts to brown. Add fresh sage leaves and let cook until beginning to crisp. Add the sage and butter to the bread mixture. Moisten with just enough stock to get the mixture to bind. Taste and adjust seasonings with salt and pepper.

Gently fill a baking dish with the stuffing. Do not pack as the stuffing needs room to expand. Bake uncovered for 30 to 45 minutes. If you prefer a softer crust, cover for the first 20 minutes.

Yield: about 7 cups

Note: To toast and skin hazelnuts, spread on a baking sheet and bake at 350° for 10 to 12 minutes or until lightly browned. Pour nuts onto a large towel. Let cool slightly, then rub together in towel to remove skins.

Bourbon Soaked Baked Beans

Cade Nagy, Executive Chef  **Paul's Catering**

1	*lb. navy beans*
1	*cup bourbon*
	About 2 1/2 cups water
1/2	*cup dark brown sugar*
1	*small yellow onion, chopped*
1/4	*lb. barbecue meat scraps (leftovers)*
1	*Tbsp. soy sauce*
1	*tsp. Worcestershire sauce*
1/2	*tsp. dry mustard*
	Salt and freshly ground black pepper

Wash beans. Place beans and bourbon in a large pan and cover with water. Bring to a boil over medium-high heat. Reduce to low heat and simmer, adding more water as necessary, (up to 2 cups more) until beans are tender, 1 to 1 1/2 hours. Drain and reserve cooking water.

Preheat oven to 275°. In a bean pot or ovenproof dish, layer beans, sugar, onion and meat scraps, ending with a layer of beans. Mix together soy sauce, Worcestershire, mustard, and salt and pepper to taste. Stir into beans. Add bean cooking water to cover. Bake, uncovered, for 5 to 6 hours.

Serves 8

Vegetables

Fennel

Vegetables

Fennel Au Gratin

Jaydee Boat  **At Home in Provence**

2	*large fennel bulbs*
1/4	*cup chicken stock*
2	*Tbsp. Lillet or Madeira*
1/2	*cup soft bread crumbs*
1 - 2	*grinds freshly grated nutmeg*
	Salt and freshly ground black pepper to taste
3/4	*cup grated Gruyére cheese*

Preheat oven to 350°.

Wash and trim fennel. In a large pot of boiling water, poach (simmer) whole fennel bulbs until almost tender. Drain. Thickly slice fennel and place in buttered gratin dish.

Pour stock and wine over fennel. Sprinkle bread crumbs, seasoning and cheese on top. Bake for 20 to 25 minutes until browned and sauce is reduced to a glaze.

Serves 6

Sautéed Greens

Conni Gallo, Chef  **Go Gourmet**

"This is easy and fast. Served as a bed under grilled fish or chicken, this vegetable really dresses up the plate. Sauté the greens as the last step before serving your meal"

2 bunches of spinach and/or lettuce and/or mixed greens of any kind, washed and patted dry
1 tsp. olive oil

In large non-stick sauté pan, heat olive oil. Add greens, season with salt and pepper, and begin moving the greens around (a pair of tongs works great for this), so that the greens all cook evenly. Remove from pan onto the serving platter or plates as soon as greens are wilted; cooking too long will lose the bright color and fresh flavor.

Serves 4

Zucchini-Tomato Fans

Conni Gallo, Chef  **Go Gourmet**

"Inspired by an eggplant dish I saw Jacques Pepin prepare at the Aspen Food and Wine Festival, I decided to create this simple, but elegant vegetable. The red and green is very colorful, and the ever-popular Mediterranean flavors mingle very nicely when paired with poultry"

1 small zucchini per person
1 small Roma tomato per person
Scant tsp. olive oil
Dash each dried basil, thyme and oregano
Salt and freshly ground black pepper to taste

Preheat oven to 350°.

Trim ends of zucchini and slice horizontally, keeping one end intact, about 5 to 6 slices. Thinly slice Roma tomato lengthwise into 5 to 6 separate slices. On a baking sheet sprayed with non-stick cooking spray, fan zucchini out and place a slice of tomato between each break in the fan.

Drizzle with olive oil and sprinkle herbs over fans. May be prepared to this point several hours in advance.

Roast about 35 minutes, until zucchini is tender. Season with salt and pepper. With a spatula, carefully remove to a serving platter or plates.

Garlic Mashers

Theo Roe, Executive Chef  **Dazzle Restaurant and Lounge**

8 russet potatoes, peeled and cut into eighths
8 garlic cloves
Kosher salt
1/2 cup (1 stick) unsalted butter
1/2 cup cream or milk
Salt and freshly ground black pepper to taste

Place potatoes and garlic in a pot. Add cold water to cover and about 1 Tbsp. kosher salt. Bring to a boil; reduce the heat to a heavy simmer. Cook until potatoes can be pierced easily with a fork; drain.

Place potatoes into a standing mixer bowl; use the paddle attachment to mash together with the butter and cream. (You can also do this by hand.) Season to taste with salt and pepper.

Serves 8 to 12

Truffled Mashed Potatoes

Chris Cina, Executive Chef  **Fourth Story Restaurant and Bar**

3 lbs. russet potatoes, peeled and quartered
2 cups half-and-half
1 cup (2 sticks) unsalted butter
3 Tbsp. truffle oil
About 1 oz. truffles, minced (or whatever you can afford)
Salt and freshly ground white pepper

Cook potatoes in boiling, salted water until tender. Meanwhile, combine half-and-half with butter in a saucepan and heat until warm.

Drain potatoes well. Place in mixer bowl with paddle attachment and mash, gradually adding warm half-and-half mixture until no more can be absorbed. Add truffle oil and minced truffles. Season to taste with salt and pepper.

Serves 6

Yukon Potato Gratin with Bacon and Smoked Cheddar Cheese

Chris Cina, Executive Chef  **The Fourth Story Restaurant and Bar**

"A nice side dish for a holiday meal; great for brunch also"

7	*Yukon Gold potatoes, peeled and sliced 1/4 inch thick*
	Butter
1 1/2	*lbs. smoked cheddar cheese, sliced or grated*
3/4	*lb. bacon, diced (preferably applewood smoked)*
3	*cups heavy whipping cream*
	Salt and freshly ground black pepper to taste

Preheat oven to 375°. Place the potatoes into a pot with cold water and slowly bring to a boil. Drain potatoes and place in cold water to cool.

Butter a 9 by 12 inch casserole dish, Add layers of potatoes and cheese until all the potatoes have been used.

In a saucepan, cook the bacon until it just begins to crisp up; add the cream and bring to a boil. Season with salt and pepper. Pour the hot cream over the potatoes and cover the dish with foil.

Bake until the potatoes become tender (about 30 minutes). Remove the foil and allow the potatoes to attain a golden brown color on top. Allow to cool slightly and serve.

Serves 8 to 10

Potato and Wild Rice Cakes

Cade Nagy, Executive Chef **Paul's Catering**

1/2 cup wild rice, uncooked
1/2 tsp. salt

2 large potatoes, peeled
3 green onions, cut on the bias
Cayenne pepper
Salt and freshly ground black pepper to taste
Oil
Additional sliced green onions for garnish

Bring 2 cups of water to a boil. Slowly stir in wild rice and salt. Simmer for 40 to 50 minutes or until tender. Drain.

Meanwhile, place potatoes in a large pot of water. Bring to a boil and cook until fork tender. Drain and chill for 2 to 3 hours until cold. Shred potatoes into a large bowl. Add cooked wild rice, sliced green onions, cayenne pepper, salt and pepper to taste. Mix well; mixture will be sticky.

Form into a 1/2 inch thick patty about the size of your palm. Sauté in hot oil until golden brown on both sides. Serve garnished with sliced green onions.

Serves 6

Sweet Potato Oven Fries

Conni Gallo, Chef  **_Go Gourmet_**

2 - 4	*large sweet potatoes*
	Olive oil
	Salt and freshly ground black pepper
	Pinch of cinnamon

Preheat oven to 400°.

Peel sweet potatoes and cut lengthwise into even sticks 1/2 inch wide. Toss with olive oil and season with salt, pepper and cinnamon. Place in a single layer on a baking sheet and cook about 20 minutes. Turn and cook on the other side until deep brown.

Serves 4

Roasted Sweet Potato Purée

Conni Gallo, Chef  **Go Gourmet**

8 small sweet potatoes (about 2 1/2 lbs.)
1/3 cup lime juice
Salt and freshly ground black pepper

Preheat oven to 400°.

Prick sweet potatoes with a fork in several places and roast on a foil-lined baking sheet in middle of the oven for 1 hour 15 minutes, or until very soft. (If the potatoes are not completely soft, they will not purée nicely.)

Cool potatoes just until they can be handled and scoop flesh into a food processor. Purée until smooth, adding a little hot water if necessary. Add lime juice, salt and pepper; purée until completely combined.

Serves 8

Broccoli and Tofu with Black Bean Sauce

Gigia Kolouch, Culinary Instructor  **The Natural Pantry**

1	*16-oz. pkg. firm tofu*
2	*heads broccoli*
1	*red pepper*
1	*bunch green onions*
Sauce:	
1	*Tbsp. cornstarch*
1/3	*cup Chinese cooking wine or dry sherry*
3	*Tbsp. Chinese soy sauce*
1/3	*cup vegetable stock*
	or l tsp. miso mixed with 1/3 cup water
2	*tsp. chili paste*
1	*Tbsp. sugar*
1	*tsp. salt*
1 1/2	*Tbsp. sesame oil*
4	*Tbsp. vegetable oil*
1	*Tbsp. minced ginger*
4	*cloves garlic, peeled and sliced*
2	*Tbsp. fermented black beans*
	Cooked rice

Cut the tofu into 1/2 inch cubes. Place the tofu in between several layers of paper towels and place a weight (like a cutting board) on top. Let stand while you prepare the rest of the meal. (This removes excess water and makes the tofu firmer.)

Cut the broccoli into long florets. Cut the red pepper into strips. Trim off the ends of the green onions. Cut into 2 inch pieces and shred each piece so you have long, thin strands of onions.

Mix together the ingredients for the sauce and set aside.

Heat the wok and add 4 tablespoons oil. When the oil is hot, add the tofu, a few cubes at a time, and stir-fry until golden brown and slightly puffed. Remove with a slotted spoon onto paper towels to drain. After all of the tofu cubes have been fried, drain some of the oil from the wok, leaving about 1 tablespoon. Add the ginger, garlic and black beans mashing the beans with a wooden spoon. Stir a few times, then add the broccoli. Cook, covered, for 1 minute. Broccoli should be bright green.

Add the red pepper and stir-fry for 1 to 2 minutes. Add the tofu and gently mix together. Stir the sauce then add to the wok. Cook, stirring, until sauce has thickened. Add the green onions and continue to cook, stirring, for 1 minute. Serve immediately over cooked rice.

Serves 4

Tempeh Tacos

Gigia Kolouch, Culinary Instructor  The Natural Pantry

"Tempeh is a hearty and delicious substitute for ground meats. In this recipe, Mexican seasonings give the tempeh a spicy flavor. Use basil and oregano in other recipes to make Italian tempeh"

for the tempeh:

2	*cups vegetable broth*
16	*oz. tempeh*
1	*medium onion, diced*
2	*cloves garlic, minced*
1	*Tbsp. oil*
1	*tsp. each ground cumin, ground coriander and oregano*
2	*tsp. chili powder*
2	*tsp. fresh lime juice*
	Salt to taste

for the garnishes:

1	*package taco shells*
1	*tomato, chopped*
1	*cup grated cheddar cheese*
2	*cups shredded lettuce or cabbage*
1/4	*cup sour cream*
1/4	*cup salsa or chile sauce*
1/4	*cup sliced green onions*

Heat the vegetable broth in a small pan. Place the tempeh in the broth and simmer gently for 20 minutes. Preheat the oven to 350°. Meanwhile, sauté the onion and garlic in oil in a large skillet. Stir in the cumin, coriander, oregano and chili powder. Sauté until onion is translucent, about 10 minutes.

When the tempeh is tender, remove it from the broth and allow to cool. Reserve the broth. Crumble the tempeh and add it to the onion mixture. Add the lime juice and salt. Simmer for 5 to 10 minutes, until the tempeh is heated through. You may need to add 1/4 cup of broth to keep the tempeh from sticking.

Place the garnishes in small bowls and place the tempeh in a serving bowl. Warm the taco shells for 5 minutes and place on a platter. Serve, letting guests fix tacos according to their own preference.

Serves 4

Sauces and More

Thyme

Sauces and More

BBQ Grilled Corn Salsa

Matt Selby, Executive Chef  **Vesta Dipping Grill**

"Great with grilled chicken"

2	*ears fresh corn, husked*
1 1/2	*cups of your favorite barbecue sauce*
	Kosher salt and freshly ground black pepper
1	*red onion, peeled and finely diced*
2	*large tomatoes, cored and finely diced*
1/2	*fresh poblano chili, finely diced*
2	*Tbsp. chopped fresh cilantro*
1	*Tbsp. chopped fresh basil*
1	*Tbsp. fresh lime juice*

Place corn in a container and cover with barbecue sauce. Sprinkle with salt and pepper, and marinate corn for at least 1 hour. If using a grill, make sure that grill is very hot, then grill all sides of corn until black grill marks appear. If not using a grill, place corn into very hot sauté pan with oil and sear all sides. Return corn to container with barbecue sauce and allow to cool.

When corn is cool enough to handle, cut corn away from the cob and place kernels in a mixing bowl. With the back of your knife, scrape the bare cobs into the bowl to get all of the sweet corn juice.

Into the same bowl, scrape the barbecue sauce from the corn container and add all of the chopped vegetables and herbs. Season with lime juice and mix thoroughly. Season to taste with salt and pepper. Feel free to add more barbecue sauce to your liking.

Yield: 2 cups

Cranberry and Dried Cherry Compote

Conni Gallo, Chef  **Go Gourmet**

8	*shallots (about 1 inch in diameter)*
2	*tsp. butter*
1/3	*cup sugar*
1/4	*cup white wine vinegar, divided*
1/2	*cup dry white wine*
1/4	*tsp. salt*
1/2	*cup dried unsweetened cherries*
1	*cup fresh or frozen (do not thaw) cranberries*
1/4	*cup water*

Blanch shallots in boiling water for 1 minute; drain and peel.

Melt butter in a saucepan and cook shallots until coated well with butter. Add sugar and 1/2 tablespoon vinegar. Cook, stirring, until sugar mixture turns a deep golden color. Add remaining vinegar, wine and salt; boil for 1 minute. Add cherries; reduce heat and simmer, covered, until shallots are tender, about 45 minutes.

Add cranberries and water. Boil gently, uncovered, about 10 minutes, stirring occasionally. Serve compote at room temperature.

Serves 4

Cranberry Sauce with Apricots and Currants

Conni Gallo, Chef — **Go Gourmet**

4 cups cranberries
2 cups sugar
1 cup roughly chopped dried apricots
1 cup currants
1 cup water
1 cup orange juice
1 Tbsp. orange zest

In large saucepan, combine all ingredients. Stir over medium heat until sugar dissolves. Cover pan and increase heat to high. Bring to a boil and cook until cranberries pop, about 8 minutes. Transfer to bowl. Cool, then cover and refrigerate until cold.

Yield: about 3 cups

Crème Fraîche

Conni Gallo, Chef  **Go Gourmet**

"Crème Fraîche can be substituted in most recipes that call for heavy cream as it can be boiled with curdling. It is also delicious served cold as a sauce over fresh fruit or other desserts"

1 *cup heavy cream (not ultra-pasteurized)*
1 *cup dairy sour cream or 2 Tbsp. buttermilk*

Combine ingredients in a glass bowl and stir well. Cover with plastic wrap and let stand at room temperature for 8 to 24 hours. The crème fraîche will be thick and creamy. Refrigerate, covered, up to 2 weeks.

Light Crème Fraîche

"Unbelievable – all the tart, creamy richness of the full-fat version, but without all the fat!"

1 *cup skim milk or non-fat half-and-half*
1 *cup non-fat or light sour cream*

Prepare as above.

Yield: 2 cups

Tip: Land O'Lakes® nonfat half-and-half and sour cream seem to work best in this low-fat version.

Dry Rub

Cade Nagy, Executive Chef  **Paul's Catering**

1 cup sugar
1/2 cup Lawry's salt
1/2 cup paprika
1/4 cup garlic salt
1/4 cup celery salt
3 Tbsp. chili powder
2 Tbsp. freshly ground black pepper
1 Tbsp. lemon pepper
2 tsp. dried sage
1 tsp. dry mustard
1/2 tsp. ground thyme
1/2 tsp. cayenne pepper

Combine all ingredients and mix well. Store in a jar. Sprinkle onto, do not rub into meat.

Yield: 3 cups

Kansas City Barbecue Sauce

Cade Nagy, Executive Chef **Paul's Catering**

1/2	*tsp. each curry powder, chili powder and paprika*
1/4	*tsp. each allspice, cinnamon, mace and freshly ground black pepper*
1/2	*tsp. hot sauce (Tabasco sauce)*
1/4	*cup white vinegar*
1/3	*cup dark molasses*
1	*cup catsup*

Sift together all dry ingredients. Combine hot sauce, vinegar, molasses and catsup. Add dry ingredients and mix well.

Store up to 3 weeks in refrigerator; up to 6 months in freezer.

Yield: 2 cups

Lime Curd

Amy Hoyt, Owner  **Heavenly Baking and Catering**

1/2	*cup (1 stick) butter*
5	*egg yolks*
1	*14-oz. can sweetened condensed milk*
1/2	*cup lime juice*
	Zest of one lime

Melt butter and keep warm. In a food processor, beat the egg yolks and milk thoroughly. With the motor running, pour in the hot butter, then add the lime juice and zest.

Chill for 2 hours to firm the curd. Store tightly covered; keeps well for up to 10 days. Delicious served with scones.

Yield: about 2 cups

Mango-Black Bean Relish

Dan Barnes, Executive Chef  **Denver Buffalo Company**

"This is a refreshing summer relish to accompany pork, chicken or fish. It can even be served warm during cooler weather"

1	*lime, zested*
2	*limes, juiced*
1/2	*cup mango purée*
1/2	*cup diced mango*
1/2	*cup cooked black beans (if using canned, rinse and drain)*
1/2	*cup peeled and diced jicama*
1/4	*cup peeled, seeded and diced cucumber*
1/4	*cup diced red bell pepper*
1/4	*cup diced red onion*
1/8	*cup finely chopped cilantro*
1	*jalapeño pepper, seeded and thinly sliced*
2	*tsp. olive oil*
	Salt and freshly ground black pepper to taste

Combine all ingredients and chill in refrigerator. Bring to room temperature before serving.

Yield: 4 cups

Pepper Catsup

Conni Gallo, Chef  **Go Gourmet**

"Delicious served with grilled steak, burgers, chicken or oven-fried potatoes"

1	*Tbsp. olive oil*
1/4	*cup diced red onion*
5	*green onions, diced*
1/2	*red bell pepper, diced*
1/2	*yellow bell pepper, diced*
I	*small jalapeño, minced*
2	*whole chipotle chiles in adobo sauce, minced*
1	*clove garlic, minced*
	Pinch dried thyme
1/2	*tsp. salt*
	Pinch cayenne pepper
1/2	*cup catsup*
1/2	*tsp. freshly ground white pepper*

Heat oil in a saucepan. Add the onions, bell peppers, chiles, garlic, thyme, salt, and cayenne. Cook the mixture over medium heat, covered, for 5 minutes. Add the catsup and white pepper; cook an additional 5 minutes or until thick.

Yield: about 1 cup

Pineapple-Citrus Chutney

Dan Barnes, Executive Chef  **Denver Buffalo Company**

"This chutney is great served with grilled or roasted pork or chicken"

1	*pineapple*
1	*Tbsp. olive oil*
1	*Tbsp. butter*
3	*cloves garlic, minced*
3	*Tbsp. minced fresh ginger*
1/2	*cup diced red onion*
1/2	*cup diced red pepper*
3/4	*cup brown sugar*
1/3	*cup red wine vinegar*
1 1/2	*cups mango pieces*
	Juice of 2 oranges

Trim top and bottom off pineapple. Stand pineapple upright and trim away rind, being careful to remove all eyes. Cut pineapple in half vertically, then cut in half again so there are 4 long pieces. Remove the hard core from each quarter. Place quarters on a grill or under a broiler and cook, turning occasionally, until well-browned on all sides. Cool and cut into 1/2 inch dice.

Heat a heavy bottomed saucepan and add olive oil, then the butter. When sizzling, add garlic, ginger, onion and red pepper. Cook about 2 minutes on medium-high heat. Add brown sugar and wine vinegar; bring to a boil. Add pineapple, mango and orange juice; simmer for 5 to 10 minutes until flavors meld.

Yield: about 2 1/2 cups

Quick Tomato Sauce

Amy Hoyt, Owner  **Heavenly Baking and Catering**

1	*onion, chopped*
3	*cloves garlic, minced*
3	*Tbsp. olive oil*
1	*28-oz. can plum tomatoes, with juice (chopped)*
1/2	*cup fresh basil leaves*
1	*tsp. dried oregano*
	Freshly ground black pepper, to taste

In a saucepan, sauté the onion and garlic in olive oil until tender and transparent. Add tomatoes, basil and oregano. Simmer for 20 to 30 minutes or until thickened. Use as a pizza topping.

Yield: about 2 1/2 cups

Spicy Ancho Tomato Sauce

Matt Selby, Executive Chef  **Vesta Dipping Grill**

"This versatile sauce can be used for marinating red meats, as well as a dipping sauce for beef, pork and chicken. It makes a great chip dip also!"

5	*ancho chilies, rehydrated in hot water*
1/2	*fresh poblano chile, chopped*
2	*fresh tomatoes, cored and chopped*
6	*whole garlic cloves, peeled*
1/2	*onion, peeled and chopped*
1	*tsp. allspice*
1	*tsp. dried thyme*
1	*tsp. dried oregano*
1	*tsp. dried marjoram*
1	*tsp. cumin*
1	*cup rehydrating water from chiles*
1	*Tbsp. red wine vinegar*
1/2	*cup (1 stick) unsalted butter, cut into pieces*
	Kosher salt and freshly ground black pepper to taste
	Lemon or lime juice (optional)

Place all ingredients, except the butter, salt and pepper in a blender or food processor. Purée on highest setting until ingredients are thoroughly blended.

Transfer ingredients to a large sauce pot and place over high heat. When sauce is hot, add the butter in pieces. Reduce heat to avoid scorching. Let simmer for about 15 to 20 minutes.

Remove sauce from heat and season to taste with salt and pepper. A dash or two of fresh lemon or lime juice is a nice touch. Serve hot or chilled.

Yield: 2 cups

Yellow Curry Sauce

Matt Selby, Executive Chef  **Vesta Dipping Grill**

"This warmly-hued sauce pairs wonderfully with grilled tuna. Try it also with chicken, beef and pork"

1/2	*cup (1 stick) unsalted butter*
1	*onion, peeled and finely diced*
1/2	*Tbsp. minced fresh garlic*
1	*Tbsp. minced fresh ginger*
1	*tsp. curry powder*
1	*tsp. cinnamon*
1	*tsp. allspice*
1	*tsp. nutmeg*
1	*tsp. coriander*
1	*tsp. cumin*
2	*cans (3 cups) coconut milk*
1	*Tbsp. fresh lemon juice*
	Kosher salt and freshly ground black pepper to taste

In a large saucepan, melt butter over medium heat until butter browns, being careful not to scorch. With pan still over medium heat, add onion, garlic and ginger; increase heat and sauté until vegetables have caramelized.

Add all dry spices to vegetables and continue to sauté until spices become extremely fragrant. Add coconut milk and bring mixture to a boil, and then simmer for about 20 minutes. Add fresh lemon juice and season to taste with salt and freshly ground black pepper.

Yield: 3 cups

Desserts and Cookies

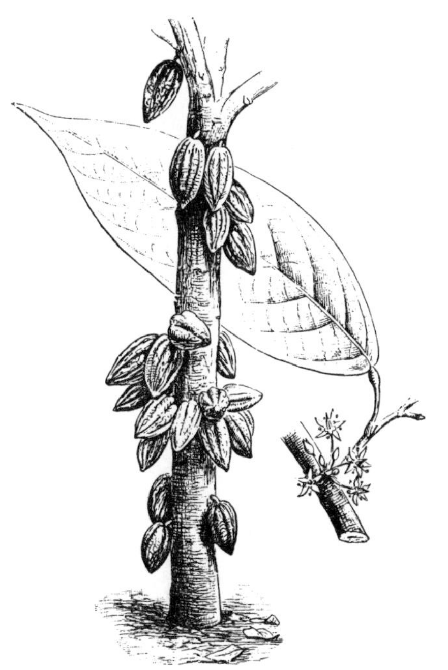

Cocoa

Desserts and Cookies

Perfect Pie Crust

Amy Hoyt, Owner  **Heavenly Baking and Catering**

2	*sticks (1 cup) butter, very cold or frozen*
2 2/3	*cups flour*
1 1/2	*Tbsp. sugar (optional)*
1/2	*cup ice water*

Place butter and flour (and sugar, if used) in a food processor with a steel blade and process until it reaches the consistency of coarse corn meal. With the motor running, add the ice water in a steady stream. Then begin pulsing the motor until the dough almost comes together.

Turn dough out onto a lightly floured surface and form into two balls. Be sure not to knead or overwork the dough as this will make it tough. Use immediately or wrap tightly and store in refrigerator for no more than 3 days. May be frozen up to a month.

To roll out pie crust, lightly flour your work surface and rolling pin. Place 1 ball of dough on floured surface and roll from center out to edge, forming a circle about 2 inches larger than your pie pan. If dough sticks to work surface, flour lightly. If dough tears press together with fingers. Fold dough in half and place in pie pan; gently press into pan taking care not to stretch dough. Fold edge under to form a rim; flute edges.

For a tart shell, use a tart pan with a removable bottom. Roll out dough (as above) about 1 inch larger than tart pan. Fold dough in half and place in tart pan. Gently press into place. Trim dough flush with top of tart pan by running the rolling pin across top of tart.

For a baked, unfilled pie or tart shell: prick bottom and sides of shell all over with a fork. Line unbaked pie shell with foil or parchment paper. Spread pie weights (or dried beans) over bottom of lined pie shell. Bake at 375° for 10 to 15 minutes. Remove weights and foil; continue baking for another 5 to 10 minutes until bottom is lightly browned. (This is called blind baking and prevents dough from bubbling up when baking.)

Yield: one (two crust) 9 inch pie or two 9 inch tart shells

Variation: add chopped nuts or citrus zest to dough for flavoring.

Graham Cracker Crust

Amy Hoyt, Owner  ***Heavenly Baking and Catering***

1 1/2	*cups graham cracker crumbs*
1/4	*cup sugar*
1	*tsp. cinnamon*
6	*Tbsp. butter, melted*

In a medium bowl, combine graham cracker crumbs, sugar and cinnamon. Stir in melted butter until well-blended. Press into a 9 inch pie pan. Bake at 350° for 10 minutes or until lightly browned.

Yield: one 9 inch pie shell

Variation: substitute chocolate wafers for graham crackers.

All Fruit Mincemeat

Amy Hoyt, Owner  **Heavenly Baking and Catering**

5	*lbs. Granny Smith apples*
1 1/2	*lbs. raisins*
1	*lb. currants*
1	*lb. brown sugar*
3/4	*lb. butter*
1/2	*lb. candied orange peel*
1	*cup cider vinegar*
1	*cup apple cider*
1/2	*cup dark molasses*
1 1/2	*tsp. cloves*
1 1/2	*tsp. nutmeg*
1 1/2	*tsp. allspice*
1 1/2	*tsp. cinnamon*
1 1/2	*cups brandy*

Peel, core and slice the apples. Place in a large pot with all ingredients, except the brandy. Bring to a boil; reduce heat and simmer for one hour. Stir frequently to prevent burning on the bottom. It will become quite dark and thick. Remove from heat and stir in the brandy. Allow to cool completely before filling pies.

Yield: enough filling for two 9 inch pies

To make a pie, use a double crust. See Apple Pie, page 215, for directions for rolling out the dough and assembling the pie. Fill with about one-half of the filling. Bake at 350° until the crust is golden brown, about 45 to 60 minutes.

Apple Pie

Amy Hoyt, Owner  **Heavenly Baking and Catering**

"Adjust the amount of sugar used according to tartness of the apples"

10	*apples, preferably Granny Smith*
3/4	*cup sugar*
1/2	*cup flour*
1/2	*tsp. cinnamon*
1/4	*tsp. nutmeg*
1	*recipe Perfect Pie Crust (page 211)*
1	*Tbsp. butter*

Preheat oven to 400°. Peel, core and thinly slice apples. Whisk together sugar, flour and spices. Add to apples and mix thoroughly, being careful not to crush or break up the apples (use your hands).

Divide pie dough into two pieces, one slightly larger than the other. To roll out pie crust, lightly flour your work surface and rolling pin. Place one piece of dough on floured surface and roll from center out to edge, forming a circle about 2 inches larger than your pie pan. If dough sticks to work surface, flour again lightly. If dough tears press together with fingers. Fold dough in half and place in pie pan; gently press into pan taking care not to stretch dough.

Pack the apples into the pie crust. You won't think you can get all the apples in the pie, but keep pressing down and shifting them around until you have a tight, high dome of apples. Dot with butter.

Roll out top crust and place on top of the apples; fold edges under to seal. Cut several slashes in the top for air vents. Decorate with dough cut outs if desired. Bake at 400° for 5 minutes, then turn oven down to 350° and continue baking for 1 hour or until apples are tender.

Yield: one 9 inch pie

Crostata di Frutti

Ben Davis, Executive Chef  **Tony's Meats and Specialty Foods**

Crust:

4	*cups flour*
1/2	*cup sugar*
1	*tsp. kosher salt*
1	*lb. (4 sticks) butter, very cold and cut into small chunks*
1/2	*cup ice water*

Filling:

1/4	*cup each sugar and flour*
1	*tsp. cinnamon*
4	*Tbsp. cold butter*
1 1/2	*lbs. baking apples: Macintosh, Rome Beauties or Golden Delicious, peeled and quartered*
1	*tsp. lemon zest*
1/2	*cup golden raisins*

Crust: In a food processor, combine the flour, sugar and salt; pulse to combine. Add the butter chunks and pulse 15 times to cut the butter into small chunks. Do not over process. With the machine running, add the water all at once and mix until the water is combined into the flour. Do not let the dough become a solid mass. Turn the dough out and shape into a disk. Wrap in foil and chill for 1 hour. Preheat the oven to 400°.

Filling: Combine the sugar, flour, cinnamon and butter with a pastry cutter, knives or your fingers until it resembles a coarse meal. Toss apples with the zest and raisins.

On a lightly floured surface, roll out the dough into 1 large crust, 2 small or 4 individual crusts. Place apples in the center of the crust, leaving a border of dough all around the edge. Sprinkle sugar-flour mixture over apples. Fold the edges of the tart dough around the edges of the apples, leaving the apples exposed in the center of the tart. Transfer to a baking sheet and bake until the dough is golden brown and the apples are soft, about 20 minutes.

Yield: 1 large, 2 small or 4 individual tarts

The lightly sparkling Moscato da Asti from the Piedmont area of Italy is a great way to liven up this dessert with its fresh melon and pear flavors. Try the Michael Chiarlo "Nivole" Moscato da Asti.

Mom's Blueberry Cream Cheese Pie

Amy Hoyt, Owner  **Heavenly Baking and Catering**

12 oz. cream cheese, room temperature
1/2 cup sugar
1 tsp. vanilla
1/3 cup sour cream
2 eggs, beaten
1 9 inch pre-baked Graham Cracker Crust (page 213)

1/2 cup red currant jelly
3 cups fresh blueberries, washed and well drained

Preheat oven to 350°.

Beat the cream cheese with a mixer until creamy. Beat in the sugar and vanilla. Add the sour cream and eggs; mix just to blend well. Pour into the pre-baked crust and bake for 25 minutes. Remove from oven and cool to room temperature. Refrigerate for at least 1 hour or overnight before topping with fruit.

Place the jelly in a medium saucepan and melt over medium heat. Bring to a boil and simmer for 1 minute. Brush a thin layer of jelly over the top of the chilled pie. Gently fold the blueberries into the remaining jelly and pour over the pie in an even layer. Refrigerate for at least 1 hour before serving.

Yield: one 9 inch pie

Spiced Pumpkin Pie

Amy Hoyt, Owner  **_Heavenly Baking and Catering_**

1/3	*cup sugar*
1 1/2	*tsp. cinnamon*
1/2	*tsp. ginger*
1/4	*tsp. cloves*
1/4	*tsp. allspice*
1/4	*tsp. cardamom*
3	*eggs*
1/3	*cup brown sugar*
1	*15-oz. can pumpkin*
1 1/4	*cups cream*
1/4	*cup milk*
1	*9 inch unbaked pie crust (page 211)*

Preheat oven to 350°.

Whisk together the white sugar and spices to break up any lumps. In a separate bowl, beat the eggs with the brown sugar and pumpkin. Beat in the spice mixture. Stir in the cream and milk.

Place dough on a lightly floured surface and sprinkle lightly with flour. Sprinkle a little flour on rolling pin also. Roll out dough from center to edge, forming a circle about 2 inches larger than your pie pan. If dough tears press together with fingers. Fold dough in half and place in pie pan; gently press into pan taking care not to stretch dough. Fold edge under to form a rim; flute edges.

Pour filling into pie shell and bake for 1 hour or until filling is set. Cool slightly before cutting.

Yield: one 9 inch pie

Banana Walnut Tart

Amy Hoyt, Owner  **Heavenly Baking and Catering**

Filling:

1 1/2	*cups walnuts*
1/2	*cup brown sugar*
4	*Tbsp. butter, softened*
2	*eggs*
3	*Tbsp. flour*
1/4	*tsp. cinnamon*
1	*Tbsp. rum (or 1 tsp. rum flavoring)*
3	*bananas, sliced*
1	*9 inch unbaked tart shell (page 211)*
	Melted chocolate or powdered sugar

Preheat oven to 350°. Place all filling ingredients (except bananas) in the bowl of a food processor and process until smooth.

Spread banana slices evenly in the bottom of the unbaked tart shell. Pour the walnut mixture over the bananas, covering them completely. Bake for 30 to 45 minutes or until golden brown and set. Allow to cool completely before serving. Garnish with melted chocolate or powdered sugar before serving.

Yield: one 9 inch tart

Variation: can also be made with pears or apples.

Bananas, walnuts and Tawny port—an instant classic. The caramel and vanilla flavors of the Tawny style of port go wonderfully with this rich dessert. Try the 10 year version from Taylor Fladgate from Portugal.

Bittersweet Chocolate Raspberry Tart

Amy Hoyt, Owner  **Heavenly Baking and Catering**

1/4	*cup milk*
2	*Tbsp. heavy cream*
1/4	*cup sugar*
1/8	*tsp. salt*
12	*oz. bittersweet chocolate, chopped*
4	*large, eggs, separated*
1	*tsp. vanilla*
1 1/2	*cups fresh raspberries*
2	*8 inch baked tart shells (page 211)*

In a heavy saucepan, heat milk, cream, sugar and salt to just below boiling. Remove from heat and stir in chocolate until smooth. Beat in egg yolks one at a time until glossy, then stir in vanilla.

In a separate bowl, beat egg whites until stiff then fold into chocolate mixture. Before egg whites are completely incorporated, gently fold in the raspberries.

Spread mixture into tart shells and chill until firm. Top with dollops of whipped cream before serving

Yield: two 8 inch tarts

For a new twist try the Renwood Ice Zin made from red grapes from Amador county in California. This rare wine will entice the palate with enormous flavor and give an emphatic flavor boost to the tart.

Lemon Blueberry Tart

Andrea Alix, Owner and Executive Chef  **Cuisine Chez Vous**

Crust:

3	*cups gingersnap cookies, finely ground*
3/4	*cup butter, melted*

Filling:

1/2	*cup sugar*
3	*Tbsp. cornstarch*
1/3	*cup water*
3/4	*cup fresh lemon juice*
1	*Tbsp. lemon zest, chopped*
2	*large eggs yolks*
2	*pints (about 4 cups) blueberries, stemmed and washed*
1/4	*cup apricot preserves*

Crust: Preheat oven to 350°. Mix together the ground gingersnaps and melted butter, mixture should hold together when squeezed in hand. Press crust into a 12 inch tart pan with a removable bottom and bake for 12 to 15 minutes. Remove and let cool completely before filling.

Filling: Combine sugar and cornstarch in medium size saucepan; mix in water, lemon juice, zest and egg yolks. Place over medium-high heat and bring to a boil, stirring constantly to prevent sticking or burning. Cook until thickened. Place lemon filling in a metal bowl, top with a piece of plastic wrap and chill for at least 1 1/2 hours.

To assemble, spread chilled lemon filling into crust and top with blueberries. Melt apricot preserves in a small saucepan, then brush onto blueberries. Let set for 5 minutes before serving.

Serves 8

Almond Polenta Pound Cake

Conni Gallo, Chef **Go Gourmet**

3/4	*cup butter, softened*
4	*oz. almond paste*
1 1/4	*cups sugar, divided*
1	*tsp. vanilla extract*
6	*eggs, separated*
1 1/2	*cups cake flour*
3/4	*cup polenta*
1	*tsp. baking powder*
1	*cup heavy cream*

Preheat oven to 350°. Grease, flour and line a 9 inch cake pan with parchment paper.

With an electric mixer, cream together butter, almond paste, 1 cup of the sugar and vanilla; scrape down sides of bowl frequently. Add egg yolks to butter mixture and beat well.

In another bowl, combine cake flour, polenta and baking powder. Add dry ingredients to butter mixture along with the heavy cream. Mix until blended; set aside.

Beat egg whites with remaining 1/4 cup sugar until soft peaks form. Fold half of the whites into the batter. Gently fold in the remaining whites and pour batter into the prepared pan. Bake for 30 minutes or until the top of the cake is golden and firm to the touch. Let the cake cool on a rack for 15 minutes before turning out of the pan. Finish cooling on the rack.

Yield: one 9 inch cake

Mara's Blueberry Bread Pudding

Mara Leone, Pastry Chef  ***janleone's***

"A delicious way to use up leftover muffins"

6	*large blueberry muffins*
9	*eggs plus 6 egg yolks*
1 1/2	*cups sugar*
1	*Tbsp. vanilla*
1 1/2	*quarts (6 cups) half-and-half*

Pre-heat oven to 350°. Crumble muffins into a 12 1/2 by 10 by 4 inch baking dish.

In a medium bowl, combine eggs, egg yolks, sugar and vanilla. Scald half-and-half over low heat. Temper (slowly mix) the egg mixture into the scalded half-and-half. Whisk together well. Pour over crumbled muffins. Place in a water bath and bake for 1 hour and 15 minutes or until a knife inserted in the center comes out clean.

Cool and refrigerate overnight. Serve with warm Caramel Sauce. May be served hot or cold. I serve it hot. Enjoy!

Serves 12

Caramel Sauce

1/2 cup butter
1 1/4 cups firmly packed brown sugar
2 Tbsp. light corn syrup
1/2 cup whipping cream

In a medium saucepan, melt butter. Stir in brown sugar and corn syrup. Bring to a boil; cook until sugar dissolves, about 1 minute, stirring constantly. Carefully stir in whipping cream and return to a boil.

Caramel Miranda

John Schenk, Owner and Executive Chef  **JKS Culinary**

Caramel:

1 1/2	*cups sugar*
2/3	*cup water*
I	*tsp. cream of tartar*
1	*cup heavy cream*
1	*Tbsp. butter*
1/4	*cup toasted coconut*
1/4	*cup pineapple, cubed*
1/4	*cup star fruit slices*
1/4	*cup raspberries*
1/4	*cup blackberries*
1/4	*cup papaya*
1/4	*cup banana, sliced*
1/4	*cup guava*
1/4	*cup mango*
3	*Tbsp. chopped white chocolate*
3	*Tbsp. chopped dark chocolate*
1 1/2	*cups macadamia nut ice cream*

Whisk together in a heavy saucepan the sugar, water and cream of tartar. Cook over medium-high heat until coppery brown. Remove from heat and carefully whisk in cream and then butter.

Preheat broiler. Drizzle caramel over an ovenproof platter. Sprinkle fruit and chocolate over caramel; broil until hot and bubbly. Spoon ice cream in the center and serve immediately.

Serves 4

Fresh Fruit with Lavender Syrup

Karin Winans  **Glen Moor Gardens**

"My favorite combination is peaches, mango, raspberries and blackberries"

Lavender Syrup:

1	*cup water*
1	*cup sugar*
2	*Tbsp. dried lavender flowers*
8	*cups of any of the following fruit in bite-size pieces: Strawberries, raspberries, blackberries, blueberries, kiwi, peaches, mango or mandarin oranges*

In a non-reactive saucepan combine all ingredients. Bring to a gentle boil, stirring until sugar dissolves, about 5 minutes. Simmer until syrup thickens, about 30 minutes. Refrigerate for 1 hour or more, until cold. Strain out flowers and mix syrup with fruit. Let stand for 30 to 60 minutes for flavors to blend before serving.

The syrup will keep well in refrigerator for at least a week.

Fresh Mango-Almond Bake

Dan Barnes, Executive Chef  **Denver Buffalo Company**

"An extremely easy recipe—perfect for the final course"

1	*cup flour*
1	*cup sugar plus 1/4 cup for mangoes*
1/2	*cup toasted blanched slivered almonds*
1 1/2	*tsp. cinnamon*
1	*egg, well beaten*
3	*lbs. fresh mangoes, peeled and cut into 1 inch pieces*
1	*stick (1/2 cup) unsalted butter, melted*

Preheat oven to 375°. Combine flour, 1 cup sugar, almonds, cinnamon and egg until crumbly. In a separate bowl, mix mango pieces with remaining 1/4 cup sugar; let stand for 5 minutes.

Place mangoes in an 8 by 12 inch baking pan and sprinkle with flour mixture. Drizzle melted butter over the crumbs. Bake for 30 minutes or until top is brown and crusty. Serve with vanilla ice cream.

Serves 6 to 8

Nothing goes better with these flavors than the world famous dessert wines from Sauterness. Try the Chateau Rieussec for a great valued French dessert wine loaded with ripe apricot and melon flavors.

Jose Cuervo® Margarita Mousse

Greg Barnhill, Executive Chef  **Three Tomatoes Catering**

"This is a beautiful dessert served in margarita glasses rimmed with sugar"

1/4	*cup lime juice*
1/4	*cup Jose Cuervo® tequila*
1	*cup sugar*
	Grated zest of two limes
1	*envelope gelatin, dissolved in 1 Tbsp. cold water*
1	*cup heavy cream, whipped to stiff peaks*
1	*cup egg whites, whipped to stiff peaks*
	Additional whipped cream for garnish, if desired
	Lime wedges and mint leaves for garnish

Heat lime juice, tequila, sugar and lime zest in a small saucepan until boiling. Mix in dissolved gelatin. Chill until almost set.

Gradually fold in whipped cream, then whipped egg whites small amounts at a time until well blended. Spoon into margarita glasses and chill before serving.

Garnish with whipped cream, lime wedge and mint leaf.

Serves 10

Zabaglione

Ben Davis, Executive Chef  **Tony's Meats and Specialty Foods**

4 egg yolks
4 egg shells of sugar or 1/4 cup
4 egg shells of Marsala or 1/2 cup
Fruit, plain sponge or pound cake

Put the egg yolks and sugar into a bowl that will fit well over a pot of simmering water. Whisk until the yolks are pale and creamy.

Place the bowl over a pot of simmering water and add the Marsala, whisking constantly. Whip the mixture until it forms soft mounds.

Zabaglione is usually served warm on top of fresh fruit or plain cake.

Serves 6

Berry-Lime Granita

Gigia Kolouch, Culinary Instructor  **The Natural Pantry**

2	*tea bags of fruit or berry tea*
1	*cup boiling water*
1/4	*cup sugar*
1	*lb. each: blackberries and strawberries, frozen or fresh*
3	*Tbsp. freshly squeezed lime juice*
2	*tsp. lime zest*
3	*Tbsp. cassis*
1/8	*tsp. salt*

Chill a 15 by 9 inch metal baking pan in the freezer. Or, if you wish to use your ice cream maker, prepare it according to the manufacturer's instructions.

Steep the tea bags in the boiling water for 5 to 10 minutes. Remove tea bags and discard. Add the sugar and simmer over medium heat until dissolved, about 5 minutes. Toss the berries with the lime juice, lime zest, cassis and salt. Pour the tea over the berries.

Transfer the mixture to a large blender or food processor and purée until smooth. You may need to do this in 2 batches. Strain the mixture through a fine mesh strainer, scraping the fruit with the back of a wooden spoon to extract as much liquid and pulp as possible. Taste for sweetness. If you need to add more sugar, dissolve it in hot water first.

Pour the mixture into the chilled baking pan and freeze until ice forms around the sides of the pan, about 30 to 45 minutes. Break up the ice crystals with a fork and stir the granita, smoothing out any large clumps. Return to the freezer. Repeat this process every 20 minutes until the granita has the consistency of a smoothie. This will take about 2 hours in most freezers (or freeze in an ice cream maker). Serve in chilled bowls.

Yield: about 2 quarts

Mango Sorbet with Fresh Raspberry Sauce

Amy Hoyt, Owner  **Heavenly Baking and Catering**

2	*mangoes*
1/2	*cup sugar*
3/4	*cup water*
	Juice of 2 limes

Peel, pit and chop the mangoes; place in food processor and process to a smooth purée. Refrigerate until ready to use.

Combine the sugar and water in a heavy saucepan and bring to a boil for 1 minute. Refrigerate until completely cool, at least 1 hour. Stir the mango purée and lime juice into the syrup and refrigerate again for at least 2 hours or overnight.

Pour mixture into an ice cream machine and freeze according to the manufacturer's directions. To serve, place about 1/4 cup Fresh Raspberry Sauce in a small bowl. Top with 2 to 3 small scoops of Sorbet and garnish with fresh raspberries. To store, pack into airtight containers and freeze for up to 2 weeks.

Yield: approximately 1 quart

Fresh Raspberry Sauce

2 1/2	*pints fresh raspberries (about 5 cups)*
1	*cup sugar, or to taste*
2	*Tbsp. fresh lemon juice*

Wash and drain raspberries. Combine with sugar and lemon juice in a small saucepan, and bring to a boil. Reduce heat and simmer for 5 minutes. Strain sauce to remove seeds. Chill before serving.

To store, cover tightly and refrigerate; keeps well for up to a week.

Yield: about 1 1/2 cups

Frozen Chocolate Mousse with Caramel Powder

Amy Hoyt, Owner  **Heavenly Baking and Catering**

2	*cups heavy whipping cream*
6	*oz. each bittersweet and unsweetened chocolate*
1/2	*cup (1 stick) butter*
5	*egg whites*
1 1/2	*cups sugar*

Place a 9 inch springform pan or 2 quart mold in the freezer. Whip the cream to soft peaks and refrigerate until needed.

Melt chocolates in a double boiler. Remove from heat and stir in butter until completely melted and blended; set aside.

Combine egg whites and sugar in the bowl of a mixer and place over a pan of simmering water. Whisk gently until the sugar dissolves and the whites are hot to the touch. Remove the bowl from the heat and whip on high speed with an electric mixer until full in volume and soft peaks form.

Quickly fold the chocolate into the meringue, then gently fold in the whipped cream. Pour into the frozen pan and smooth the top. Freeze at least 4 hours. Unmold onto a serving platter and dust with Caramel Powder.

Serves 12

Caramel Powder

1	*cup sugar*
1/2	*cup water*

Combine sugar and water in a heavy saucepan and bring to a boil. Do not stir after the mixture begins to boil or the sugar will crystallize. Brush down sides of pan with a pastry brush dipped in water to prevent sugar crystals from forming. Allow to boil briskly until the sugar reaches a deep amber color.

Remove from heat immediately and carefully pour onto a rimmed metal baking sheet. Allow to cool completely. Break the caramel into pieces and place in a food processor fitted with a steel blade. Process into a fine powder. Store tightly covered.

Oranges with Cinnamon and Chocolate

Conni Gallo, Chef  **_Go Gourmet_**

4	*medium oranges*
1 1/2	*tsp. sugar*
1/4	*tsp. cinnamon*
	Pinch cayenne pepper
1/2	*oz. finely shaved bittersweet chocolate*

Working over a bowl, prepare orange supremes (sections) by peeling orange and carefully cutting orange sections from between membranes. Squeeze the juice from the remaining pulp into the bowl. Stir in the sugar, cinnamon and cayenne. Cover and chill, up to 2 hours.

Spoon oranges and juice into individual bowls and sprinkle with shaved chocolate.

Serves 4

Pears Baked with Red Wine

Ben Davis, Executive Chef  **Tony's Meats and Specialty Foods**

1 vanilla bean, split
1 lemon
6 ripe pears
3 Tbsp. superfine sugar

Caramel:

1 1/2 cups superfine sugar
1/2 cup water
3/4 cup red wine

3 Tbsp. brown sugar
1/4 cup balsamic vinegar
Crème Fraîche (see page 198) or sour cream

Preheat the oven to 350°. Scrape seeds from vanilla bean into a small bowl. Remove zest from lemon in strips, then juice lemon. Set aside.

Slice off the bottom of the pear to allow it to stand upright. Remove core from pear from the bottom without removing the stem. Place a strip of lemon zest, 1/2 tablespoon of sugar and some vanilla seeds inside each pear. Arrange the pears upright in a baking dish. Sprinkle with lemon juice, cover with foil and bake for 10 minutes or until all the juice has been absorbed. Remove the foil.

To make the caramel: gently heat the sugar and water together to melt the sugar, then bring to a boil. Continue to boil gently until the caramel is very dark. Remove from heat. Slowly and carefully add the wine (the caramel will splatter). Pour over the pears and bake for 40 more minutes, basting every 10 minutes until the pears are wrinkled.

Remove from the oven and sprinkle with the brown sugar and balsamic vinegar. Serve with Crème Fraîche or sour cream.

Serves 6

Anise Seed Cookies

Ben Davis, Executive Chef  **Tony's Meats and Specialty Foods**

2	*cups (4 sticks) butter, softened*
1	*cup granulated sugar*
1/2	*cup powdered sugar*
4	*oz. almond paste*
3	*eggs*
1	*Tbsp. vanilla*
1	*Tbsp. anise seed*
6	*cups flour*

Preheat oven to 350°. Line cookie sheets with parchment paper.

Cream butter, sugars and almond paste. Add the eggs and vanilla; beat until smooth. Add the anise seeds and stir in the flour.

Chill the dough until it is no longer warm and can be rolled easily. Roll into a large rectangle about 1/2 inch thick. Cut with a knife dipped in flour into 1 by 1 inch squares. Place on cookie sheets and bake for about 8 to 10 minutes, or until golden brown.

Yield: about 4 dozen

Chocolate Crackle Cookies

Conni Gallo, Chef  **Go Gourmet**

1/2 cup flour
1/2 cup sugar
1/4 cup unsweetened Dutch-process cocoa
1/2 tsp. baking powder
1/4 tsp. salt
2 Tbsp. unsalted butter, softened
1 egg, lightly beaten
Powdered sugar

Preheat oven to 400°. Lightly coat cookie sheets with non-stick cooking spray.

In a stainless steel bowl, combine flour, sugar, cocoa, baking powder and salt. Blend in butter using fingers. Stir in egg until mixture is just combined. Spread dough in a thin layer in bowl and freeze for 10 minutes or until firm.

Spoon level teaspoonfuls of dough onto waxed or parchment paper. Place 2 tablespoons of powdered sugar into a small bowl and dust hands with additional powdered sugar. Roll each piece of dough into a ball and then roll in the powdered sugar. Place balls 2 inches apart on prepared cookie sheets and bake in upper and lower thirds of the oven. Switch baking sheets halfway through baking time. Bake for 8 to 10 minutes or until cookies are just set. Cool cookies on racks.

Yield: about 2 dozen

Homemade Oreos

Amy Hoyt, Owner  **Heavenly Baking and Catering**

1 1/2	cups butter, softened
2	cups sugar
2	tsp. vanilla
2	eggs
6	oz. unsweetened chocolate, melted
6	cups flour
1/2	tsp. baking powder
1/2	tsp. salt
	Cream Filling (see next page)

Preheat oven to 350°. Line cookie sheets with parchment paper or spray lightly with cooking spray.

Cream together butter and sugar with vanilla. Beat in eggs, then add the melted chocolate and blend well.

In a separate bowl, sift together the flour, baking powder and salt; add gradually to the butter mixture, blending well. Divide dough in half and roll each half into logs about 12 inches long and 1 1/2 to 2 inches in diameter. Wrap in plastic and refrigerate for 1 to 2 hours or until firm enough to slice without flattening the log.

Cut dough into 1/4 inch slices and place on cookie sheets. (If desired, mark half of the cookies with a design from a cookie press, or score with a fork.) Bake for 10 to 12 minutes. Remove to a rack to cool completely. When cool, sandwich 2 cookies together with Cream Filling.

Cream Filling

1 1/3	*cups butter, softened*
6	*cups powdered sugar*
1	*tsp. almond or mint flavoring*
3 - 5	*Tbsp. half-and-half*

Cream butter, sugar and flavoring together. Gradually add the half-and-half, and beat filling until smooth and spreadable.

Yield: 2 to 3 dozen

Variation: for ice cream sandwiches, make cookies into large rounds and replace Cream Filling with ice cream; freeze. For a Valentine's Day treat, cut with a heart-shaped cookie cutter and fill with strawberry ice cream.

Linzer Thumbprints

Amy Hoyt, Owner  **Heavenly Baking and Catering**

1	*cup butter, softened*
2/3	*cup sugar*
1	*cup finely ground hazelnuts (ok to leave skins on)*
2	*large egg yolks*
1	*tsp. vanilla*
1	*Tbsp. lemon zest*
2	*cups flour*
1	*tsp. baking powder*
1/4	*tsp. salt*
	Seedless raspberry jam
	Powdered sugar

Preheat oven to 350°. Line cookie sheets with parchment paper or spray lightly with cooking spray.

Cream together butter, sugar and the ground hazelnuts. Beat in egg yolks, vanilla and lemon zest.

In a separate bowl, sift together the flour, baking powder and salt; add gradually to the butter mixture blending well. Scoop 1 inch balls of dough onto cookie sheets and make a depression in the middle of each with your thumb. Using a small spoon, fill each with about 1/2 teaspoon of jam.

Bake for 12 minutes or until golden brown. Let cool slightly on cookie sheets, then remove to a cooling rack to cool completely Sprinkle lightly with powdered sugar.

Yield: 2 to 3 dozen

Note: the key to a light, flaky butter cookie is in the creaming stage. The butter and sugar should be creamed until they become very pale and resemble mayonnaise. If you are using a standing mixer, you can cream the butter and sugar while you gather the remaining ingredients for the recipe.

Soft Pumpkin Oatmeal Drops

Amy Hoyt, Owner — **Heavenly Baking and Catering**

3/4	*cup butter, softened*
1 1/2	*cups sugar*
2	*eggs*
1	*cup pumpkin*
1	*tsp. vanilla*
1 1/2	*cups flour*
2	*tsp. baking powder*
1/2	*tsp. each baking soda and salt*
1	*tsp. cinnamon*
1/2	*tsp. nutmeg*
	Pinch cloves
1 1/2	*cups quick oats*
1/2	*cup each shredded coconut and chopped pecans*

Preheat oven to 350°. Line cookie sheets with parchment paper or coat lightly with cooking spray.

With an electric mixer, cream together butter and sugar. Add eggs, one at a time, beating well after each addition. Stir in the pumpkin and vanilla.

In a separate bowl, sift together the flour, baking powder, baking soda, salt and spices. Mix in the quick oats. Add dry ingredients to the creamed mixture, mixing until well blended. Stir in the coconut and pecans.

Drop by tablespoonfuls (or use a small ice cream scoop) onto prepared cookie sheets. Bake for 10 to 15 minutes or until golden brown on the bottoms. Let cool slightly on cookie sheets, then remove to a rack to cool completely. Store in an airtight container; will stay soft for days.

Yield: 2 to 3 dozen

Variation: other tasty additions, in place of or in addition to the coconut, are chocolate chips, dried cranberries, raisins or currants.

Sugar Plums

Amy Hoyt, Owner — ***Heavenly Baking and Catering***

1/2 cup pecans
1/2 cup dried apricots
1/4 cup dried figs
1/4 cup golden raisins
1/4 cup coconut
2 - 3 Tbsp. orange liqueur
1/4 cup sugar

Finely chop the pecans, dried fruits and coconut in a food processor. Turn mixture into a bowl and mix in the liqueur. Form into 1 inch balls and roll in sugar. For an attractive presentation, place in mini-muffin cups.

Keep refrigerated until ready to serve or give away. The sugar plums will keep well tightly covered for one month.

Yield: about 24

ANDREA ALIX has an adventuresome spirit reflected by her extensive travel and in the creative way she combines foods. Her education at Johnson and Wales University culinary program, and her vast professional experience have led to her eclectic culinary style, a fusing and blending of flavors from around the world. After spending several years developing recipes and menus as Corporate Sous Chef for the Larimer Restaurant Group (Josephina's, Champion Brewing, Mexicali Cafe, and Cadillac Ranch), Andrea became Executive Chef at Tommy Tsunami's Pacific Diner. Currently, Andrea's company, Cuisine Chez Vous, provides catering and personal chef services.

DAN BARNES passion for food developed in his family's Iowa diner, where he began his career at the age of nine, and worked his way through the "Culinary School of Hard Knocks". He honed his skills in a variety of restaurants in Florida for eight years before moving to Denver in 1992. Dan has demonstrated his versatility working with the Larimer Group as chef at Josephina's, Champion Brewing Company, Cadillac Ranch and Tommy Tsunami's. Currently he is Executive Chef at The Denver Buffalo Company.

GREG BARNHILL, Executive Chef for Three Tomatoes Catering, brings a zest and enthusiasm to his signature culinary style that reflects his passion for creating deliciously upscale dishes. Previously, he was Executive Chef at California Cafe in Park Meadows. He has received national acclaim for creating the unique "CaliFlorida" cuisine for Ft. Lauderdale's California Cafe. Recognized for his eclectic fusion of many styles of food. Greg's professional training is highlighted by a three-year apprenticeship under The Culinary Institute's Klaus Mitterhauser. Additional experience includes The Registry Hotel, The Landing, and Chef/Owner of the Wine Cellar in Ft. Collins.

JAYDEE BOAT is the owner of At Home in Provence, a company that offers tours exploring the food, wine, art, history, culture and customs of France. Her experience in the culinary world includes cooking school teacher and director (Toddy's Market), cookbook editor (*Colorado Cache, America's Best Cookbook* and *Dining in Denver)* and founding chair of the Colorado Chapter of the American Institute of Wine and Food.

CHRISTOPHER CINA, Executive Chef of the Fourth Story Restaurant, is a 1992 graduate of the Culinary Institute of America. Christopher honed his skills with Kevin Taylor at Zenith and at Jeremiah Tower's famed Stars in Palo Alto. His contemporary American fare, derived from the classical tradition, is informed and updated by his belief that the best dishes come from the freshest foods.

MARY CLARK and her husband, Fred Bramhall, own the deliciously successful Bluepoint Bakery. Prior to this Mary was at the helm of Bluepoint Restaurants and Catering, known for excellent food influenced by world flavors. Mary was Executive Chef at Tante Louise as well as Brendle's, Denver's first "New American" Restaurant. Her career was inspired by Lynne Kasper.

WAYNE CONWELL expresses his love of Japanese food and culture as Sushi Bar Manager at Japon where he creates and oversees outstanding sushi and Japanese dishes. His interest began in college, spending a year in a Study Abroad Program in Japan. After graduation, he developed his culinary skills working for eight years at Sushi Den.

BEN DAVIS is the Executive Chef at Tony's Meats and Specialty Foods, where he oversees their kitchens and creates fabulous dishes for gourmet take-out. Previously, Ben was executive chef at Panzano's and at Mel's Bar and Grill. This Colorado native studied at the California Culinary Academy and has worked with acclaimed chefs in the Bay area. He furthered his culinary education by traveling and cooking throughout Europe. Ben's thorough instruction conveys his expertise and his passion for fine food.

SCOTT ELLIOTT is currently Executive Chef at the Executive Tower Hotel where he oversees their restaurant as well as 19 banquet rooms. A graduate of the Culinary Arts Program of the Colorado Institute of Art, he was previously Executive Chef at Starfish, renowned for its outstanding seafood. Further experience includes Mel's Bar and Grill and Pour La France Catering.

MATTHEW FRANKLIN, Executive Chef and partner of 240 Union, started his culinary career as a dishwasher, but quickly traded in his plastic apron for a chef's coat as he discovered the allure of cooking. After years of hands-on experience, he opened his first restaurant, Fresco, in Santa Fe. His talent attracted the notice of Jimmy Schmidt who brought him to the Rattlesnake Club where he honed his skills. At 240 Union his innovative cooking turned the former fish house into a showcase of contemporary American cuisine.

CONSTANCE GALLO spent 18 years in the financial industry before recognizing that cooking was her true calling. She began by cooking at Court House, a home for abused and abandoned girls. As the owner of Gallo's Galley, a purveyor of Caribbean spices, she taught cooking classes and authored the cookbook *The Traveling Chef – Low Fat Recipes You Can Make Anywhere.* After earning a degree in Culinary Arts and Sciences and Restaurant Management from Scottsdale Culinary Institute, she began teaching. Hundreds of beginning as well as advanced students at The Seasoned Chef have benefited from Conni's excellent teaching skills which helped them develop and refine their culinary expertise.

DAN HAYES, owner and Executive Chef of Campana Catering, began his culinary training early by growing up in a large Italian family. Inspired by memories of delicious meals, he pursued a career in catering and worked for 8 years for some of the finest chefs in the Colorado catering industry. Combining his passion for good food with 13 years experience as an art director and graphic designer gives him a unique perspective on food preparation and presentation.

AMY HOYT began her culinary career working at Strings and Zenith. In 1991 she opened the delicious Bobby Dazzler Bakery. Named Best of Westword in 1993, 1994 and 1995, her bakery was famous for its breads, wedding cakes and sumptuous desserts. Many of her favorites are from old-fashioned Hoyt family recipes. Amy has shared her culinary and baking expertise with hundreds of grateful students at The Seasoned Chef.

GIGIA KOLOUCH describes holiday meals with her Italian family as an "ecstasy of food and companionship". This early exposure to the communal aspects of food led her to pursue a career revolving around all aspects of food. She teaches cooking and nutrition to all ages, writes food related articles, develops curriculum, helps plan special diets and will redesign your pantry for better health and nutrition as well! She specializes in ethnic cuisine which lends spice and zest to her vegetarian classes. Her culinary versatility is endless as evidenced by her always-popular class "Cooking Without Recipes".

JANETTE LEONE, owner and Executive Chef of janleone's Restaurant, honed her culinary skills in a variety of restaurants here in Denver: Cafe Giovanni, Cafe Janette, Tabor Grill, Janique Restaurant and Siena. Her cooking is grounded in the classic style, but informed and inspired by current trends in gourmet food and dining. Experience and confidence are evident in her award-winning cuisine. Jan believes "Cooking is one of the most difficult professions. You have to have a passion for it!"

MARA LEONE, Jan's daughter, does double duty as Pastry and Sous Chef with her mom at janleone's Restaurant. Mara has the restaurant business in her blood, having also worked with her dad at Cucina Leone. Self-taught, she has garnered critical acclaim for her outstanding desserts. Pastries are her passion!

JOHN MENDES has developed and refined his culinary skills at many fine restaurants in Denver. He began at Moondance, then moved on to La Couple, Bella Ristorante, Teresa's and California Café in Park Meadows. Currently, he is the chef at The Old Stone Church in Castle Rock.

CADE NAGY, Executive Chef at Paul's Catering, is a two-time silver medal winner in the U.S. Chef's Open—the "Olympics" of Culinary Arts. He acquired award-winning knowledge and experience through studies at the American Culinary Federation. He has worked at the Ritz Carlton, The Polo Golf and Country Club and the renowned Van Gogh's in Atlanta. Cade's trademark is creativity: "I never use a recipe". He encourages students to cook from the heart and "create, create, create".

NORMA NUNEZ and her husband Nabor started La Cueva in Aurora over 25 years ago and have been serving great Mexican food ever since. La Cueva features authentic family recipes from the Guanajuato region in Mexico—and has become one of the most popular Mexican restaurants in Denver. In addition to nourishing bodies with good food, Norma believes in nourishing minds. She founded The Nuñez Foundation which supports the Bright Lights Scholarship Program, Ballet Folklorico Aurora and the Folklorico Aurora Summer Day Camp. In 1998 she won the Channel 2 *Woman of the Year* award.

JILL RICHTER, is currently working on special projects for Jax Fish House where she was formerly Executive Chef at the LoDo restaurant. In 1996, Jill graduated from the Colorado Institute of Art's School of Culinary Arts with national honors to top off a cooking career which included catering and working at such fine establishments as The Highland's Garden Cafe, The Harvest Restaurant and Bakery, Telluride's San Sophia and The Vineyard Wine Shop. Her culinary focus is preparing food that reflects the freshest and most healthful ingredients available, fusing all styles of food from Mediterranean, Provençal, Southwestern and Asian cuisines.

THEO ROE, Dazzle partner and Executive Chef, began his cooking career early—in his grandmother's kitchen. After graduating from the prestigious Culinary Institute of America, he worked at many fine restaurants including Café Luxembourg in New York City, Mustard's Grill in Napa and Michael's' On East in Florida, one of the top restaurants in the state. At Dazzle, his culinary talent is evident in his artfully crafted menus brilliantly reflecting the bounty of the seasons. His food is prepared with a subtle combination of complementary tastes and textures.

CHRISTOPHER ROWE , Director of Wine Education for Southern Wine and Spirits, discovered his passion for wine after visiting the glorious vineyards of Europe. He has a degree in Hotel and Food Administration from Boston University, attended the Chicago Wine School and studied under the Master Sommelier at the Pump Room. As a Certified Sommelier Chris has developed award-winning wine lists and educational programs for numerous restaurants. He judged wines at the Chicago Beverage Testing Institute for reviews appearing in The Wine Enthusiast magazine.

JOHN SCHENK, owner of JKS Culinary, began his training in Eugenie les Bains, France under the expertise of Michel Guerard. Upon returning to America, John honed his European knowledge as sous chef and pastry chef at the Lodge at Keystone, and as executive chef of Kilgore Trout's in Evergreen. In 1985 he successfully pioneered the concept of gourmet carry-out at J. Williams Cafe in Bergen Park. Once again, John is on the cutting edge of the culinary industry with his personal chef and catering service.

MATT SELBY, Executive Chef at Vesta Dipping Grill, considers his work in the kitchen "play" as he flexes his culinary imagination to create lively sauces and dishes layered with flavor. He began his career working long hours at Jimmy Schmidt's Rattle Snake Grill, where he developed his cooking skills, palate and culinary intuition. Matt's talent has been recognized nationally and locally, including Zagat, Westword and 5280 magazine.

KEVIN TAYLOR is nationally known for his creative, unpretentious approach to American cuisine. He has been cooking for more than half of his life, first as an apprentice at a Denver country club and for the last 14 years at his own restaurants: Zenith, Dandelion, Brasserie Z, Palettes and the newest in Hotel Teatro, Jou Jou and Kevin Taylor's. Kevin is the recipient of numerous awards for his innovative cuisine and fine restaurants.

CAROL ANN WEST has cooked professionally for over 14 years in many of Denver's finest restaurants such as Tante Louise and European Cafe. A private chef and caterer, her focus is on quality cuisine that is healthful, low in fat, and rich in flavor! Offering expert cooking instruction, she is tops at inspiring students to cook creatively and healthfully.

KARIN WINANS is a culinary herbalist who enjoys growing specialty produce and preparing food fresh from the garden. Her extensive experience includes teaching gardening and culinary classes at the Denver Botanic Gardens and various community centers, catering and special event planning at the Gardens, and writing and speaking about herbs and heirloom vegetables. She is founder and past president of the Herb Society of America-Rocky Mountain Unit, and helped start the Denver chapter of the Chefs Collaborative 2000.

THOM WISE has enjoyed a varied career, always "on stage" in some capacity. He has been an actor, taught drama, produced night club entertainment and was part-owner of Dudley's restaurant. He was theatre and restaurant critic for the *Rocky Mountain News.* as well as being the first restaurant critic for *5280* magazine. Thom also hosted a weekend food and entertainment show on KOA and KHOW radio for over eight years. He recently finished his third trip around the world, ceating his way through South America and South Africa. To date, he has visited more than 45 countries on five continents.

Kitchen Savvy

As fun and creative as cooking can be, it can also become drudgery. Our chefs were glad to share some of their tips and hints that make life in the kitchen easy, efficient and fun!

- "Mis en place" means assembling all of your ingredients before beginning to prepare a recipe. Read the recipe carefully, then measure and prep all of the ingredients before you start to cook.

- Accurate measuring is important for consistent results. Measure dry ingredients, such as flour and sugar, in dry measuring cups. Measure liquids in glass cups. Careless measuring often results in disasters!

- Store flour and sugar in wide-mouth containers for easy measuring. To measure flour accurately, spoon into a dry measuring cup, then scrape off excess with a knife or flat spatula. Don't pack flour into the measuring cup or you will have too much.

- For best results, preheat oven before baking.

- Keep your knives sharp to make cutting and chopping easier. For safety, put a damp towel under the board to prevent it from slipping while you chop.

- To keep a bowl stable on the counter while you mix, put it in a towel "ring". Fold a towel into a triangle, then fold into a narrow strip. Form into a circle, then put your bowl in the center to keep it from sliding.

- Use parchment paper to line baking sheets rather than greasing the pan. The paper can be used for several batches of cookies before discarding. A quick rinse and the baking sheet is ready to put away!

- Use a small ice cream scoop for evenly sized cookies. Dip in cold water to help the batter slide out easily. Faster and neater than the old method of using a teaspoon and scraping the batter off with your finger.

- Microwave honey for a few seconds to make it easier to pour and measure. Rinsing the measuring cup with hot water before measuring the honey will also help it slide out more easily. Or measure oil first, then the honey.

- Tongs are a great all-around kitchen tool. Use them to turn meat at a safe distance from the heat and spattering fat, lift hot pans and lids, remove food from boiling water and serve pasta or salad.

- Coat a grater lightly with nonstick cooking spray before grating cheese. Cheese doesn't stick and clean up is easier.

- Spray your chef's knife with non-stick cooking spray before cutting up dried fruit for easier chopping.

- To easily chop or mince an onion, cut in half vertically, keeping root end intact. Peel. Lay flat side on cutting board. Slice the onion lengthwise into parallel cuts, then slice horizontally.

- Store leftover onion tightly wrapped in refrigerator for up to 5 days.

- Leftover chopped onion can be frozen, then added to dishes without thawing. To sauté, thaw and pat dry first.

- To easily remove skins from tomatoes, peaches and other fruit, score the bottom with an X, then immerse in boiling water (10 seconds for a tomato, 15 seconds for a peach). Cool in ice water and peel.

- Mangoes can be tricky and dangerous to peel. Cut a slice off of the bottom end so the mango will sit flat on a work surface. Starting at the top, use a sharp paring knife to remove the skin in strips from top to bottom. Cut along the flat side of the pit to remove the fruit, then chop or cut into slices.

- Use a melon baller to remove the core and blossom end from a pear.

- Perfect orange segments are a beautiful addition to salads and other dishes. To segment, cut a slice off of the top and bottom of the orange, Then, working from top to bottom, slice the peel and white pith cleanly from the flesh. Follow the shape of the orange as you cut. Working over a bowl to catch the juice, cut between membranes to remove segments. Squeeze juice from membranes when through.

- Eggs are easiest to separate when cold; the whites beat up to greatest volume at room temperature.

- Toast nuts and seeds in a dry skillet over medium heat, shaking frequently. Watch carefully as nuts (especially pine nuts) burn easily. Remove as soon as you see a nice golden brown color. Or toast in a 350° oven for 5 to 10 minutes

- Use separate cutting boards for meat and poultry than you use for vegetables; prevents cross contamination. Or chop vegetables before using the board for meat and poultry. Always wash boards thoroughly with hot, soapy water after each use. Rub with mineral oil periodically to keep wooden boards from drying out.

Index

A

B

G

H

I

J

O

P

Q

S

V

W

Y

Z

The Best of The Seasoned Chef

Please send me _____ copies at $24.95 per book $________

Postage and handling at $3.00 per book $________

Denver-Metro residents add $1.85 tax per book $________

Colorado residents outside the Denver-Metro area add $.75 per book $________

TOTAL $________

Name ____

Address ____

City ______________________ State ________ Zip ________

Please charge my ☐ VISA ☐ MasterCard

Card Number: ______________________ Exp. Date __________

Cardholder's Signature: ______________________________

Make checks payable to: **The Seasoned Chef Cooking School**
Please do not send cash; sorry, no CODs
Send to: **The Seasoned Chef Cooking School**
999 Jasmine Street, Suite 100
Denver, C0 80220

This is your mailing label. Please print mailing information clearly.

The Seasoned Chef
Cooking School

999 Jasmine, Suite 100
Denver, CO 80220

Ship To:

____

____

____

____

The Best of The Seasoned Chef

Please send me _____ copies at $24.95 per book $________

Postage and handling at $3.00 per book $________

Denver-Metro residents add $1.85 tax per book $________

Colorado residents outside the Denver-Metro area add $.75 per book $________

TOTAL $________

Name ____

Address ____

City ____________________ State ________ Zip ________

Please charge my ☐ VISA ☐ MasterCard

Card Number: ____________________ Exp. Date ________

Cardholder's Signature: ____

Make checks payable to: **The Seasoned Chef Cooking School**
Please do not send cash; sorry, no CODs
Send to: **The Seasoned Chef Cooking School**
999 Jasmine Street, Suite 100
Denver, C0 80220

This is your mailing label. Please print mailing information clearly.

The Seasoned Chef
Cooking School
Instruction for the Novice and Advanced

999 Jasmine, Suite 100
Denver, CO 80220

Ship To:

____

____

____

____

The Best of The Seasoned Chef

Please send me ______ copies at $24.95 per book $________

Postage and handling at $3.00 per book $________

Denver-Metro residents add $1.85 tax per book $________

Colorado residents outside the Denver-Metro area add $.75 per book $________

TOTAL $________

Name ____

Address ____

City ______________________________ State ________ Zip ________

Please charge my ☐ VISA ☐ MasterCard

Card Number: ______________________________ Exp. Date ____________

Cardholder's Signature: ______________________________

Make checks payable to: **The Seasoned Chef Cooking School**
Please do not send cash; sorry, no CODs
Send to: **The Seasoned Chef Cooking School**
999 Jasmine Street, Suite 100
Denver, C0 80220

This is your mailing label. Please print mailing information clearly.

The Seasoned Chef
Cooking School
Instruction for the Novice and Advanced

999 Jasmine, Suite 100
Denver, CO 80220

Ship To:

____

____

____

____